Incense Tree

T0083580

Incense Tree
Collected Poems of Louise Ho

With an Afterword by Douglas Kerr

香 港 大 學 出 版 社
HONG KONG UNIVERSITY PRESS

Hong Kong University Press
14/F Hing Wai Centre
7 Tin Wan Praya Road
Aberdeen
Hong Kong

© Louise Ho 2009

ISBN 978-962-209-054-5

Secure On-line Ordering
http://www.hkupress.org

British Library Cataloguing-in-Publication Data
A catalogue record for this book is available
from the British Library.

Printed and bound by United League Graphic & Printing Co. Ltd., in Hong Kong, China

Contents

Acknowledgements

First and foremost, I wish to acknowledge my debt to Douglas Kerr, who first aired the idea of my collected poems and who saw to it that the idea materialized. He has also very kindly offered to provide an Afterword.

Another active supporter has been Page Richards who has been superlatively generous with her time and energy towards bringing about this volume.

To both my deeply felt gratitude.

I acknowledge collectively my thanks to editors of literary journals and those of anthologies who have published some of the poems included here. Certainly my thanks to the publishers of the three books collected here. The last section, New Poems, has not appeared as a book before.

The short preface and the two introductions to the three books are reprinted in the Appendix. I am grateful to Ackbar Abbas and Michael Hollington for allowing their inclusion.

Louise Ho

Sheung Shui Pastoral 1977

To Mary Visick and Ian McLachlan

Hong Kong Riots I, 1967

At five this morning
The curfew lifted.
Receding, it revealed
Shapes that became people
Moving among yesterday's debris.
Stones, more so than words
Are meaningless,
Out of context.

Off the Train at Sheung Shui

The evening, mellowed
By pink skies, cooled
By early summer rain
Sighs and is still.
Dark wet trunks
Hush far flung canopies,
Young leaves lush in vibrant green.
No wonder the Chinese love jade.

Pop Song I: "At Home in Hong Kong"

Feet that paddle in the shallows
Hands that sieve through slimy weeds
Eyes that reflect the thousand lights
Give but secondary sensations.
The toes are booted
The fingers are gloved
Eyes are shaded.
We talk of cultural vacuity,
We also talk of flux and instability.
The more sophisticated talk of inevitabilities,
And thus to smooth all inconsistencies.
Nevertheless we walk firmly
Though we walk on stilts,
Because we walk only
Where stilts are safe.
Schooled in our system of indirect transmissions,
We run like clock work,
And go on ticking till we stop on the dot.

Pop Song II: "I Am of Hong Kong"

One has to be so vulgar
To live in vulgar times
In vulgar places.
Where they force themselves on you
Landing on your lap
On moving buses.
Too many bodies
We have here.
The trouble is
They are alive.
Dead, they could be buried.
But the fantasia of bodily stench
Is a mere dance, almost an abstraction.
Reality is which elbow
To use, whose elbow
To avoid.
Have piecemeal what piecemeal can,
Heaven and earth conspire the moment.
Have, get, make, what I will, I must:
Minute elegance of much
Washed in gutters
Near resettlement areas
By the Carlton Hotel
Seeps into our guts
And makes Hong Kong what it is.

Sheung Shui Pastoral

Three figures,
One man and two women,
Appeared,
With white hats on their backs.
Three black figures,
Etched against a tawny sunset,
By a country road,
With plastic slippers on.
Their new hats in
Tightly woven straw,
Milky white against their black peasant suits.
Clean and inhuman
They pressed forward
With methodical tread
Into the sunset
Like figures splashed on some bill board
Advertising acrylic colours.
Paints that do not mix or blend,
That cannot hide the crudity of flat monochromes.
(One must not puke at cheap adverts
Seeing how well they can mirror life)
One woman held the man's wrist
For support. She seemed to limp
A little: the register of a limp,
Not its helplessness. She showed
That self-reliance
Old peasant women sometimes have.
On they went
Their measured way
From nowhere to nowhere.
What secret is yours,
You dark people who follow the sun?

Babies and Mothers
(at Tai Po Train Station)

Young women
stare through space
as if counting time
like drops of rain.
Babies
in their arms
lollop round
burdened breasts
sucking thumbs.
They bawl
as they hit
the ground,
having fallen
through opened knees.

Writing Is Bleak

Writing is bleak,
Writing in this language in this place
Is doubly bleak.
How the heart yearns
For the Paris of Joyce,
Synge, Pound, Yeats,
For the camaraderie of letters
In the city of letters.

The cold night wore on.
The North wind
Riding on a country air
From some distant flute
Told me not to fret
Over the right word
Or the heart
In the right place,
That all things shall be well,
Given time.
It was singing of man's impermanence
And all his arts'.

Summer at Warwick

pheasants call
thistles listen
the air echoes
perhaps of things
from the other side of silence

in voiceless Hong Kong
we dry up from year to year
until we shrivel into dust
as people do
and produce more dust
in future generations
when will the deluge come

Boston, First Impressions (and Therefore a Bit Raw)

In the new Byzantium
Post boxes are green! *
Red brick pavements on a wet evening
Recall an older world
Cut off from
And yet of
Europe . . .
That night Seiji Ozawa
Stamped the Kabuki steps
While Mahler and Bach
Bowed to him
In formal Japanese fashion.
Angular and abrupt
Melody turns Mondrian, or Klee,
As his elbows and knees
Quiz us with geometry.
The square frames of the doors marked EXIT
Glowed in mellow light and became warm.

* *Bleary-eyed and tired, the first post box I saw did appear green. In any case, green is a good colour; it's nicely eerie.*

The John Hancock from the Top of the Prudential

A current through the dry air
Electrifies sparks, and Boston floats
On a sea of lights.
Floods of traffic swarm at our feet;
At this height we seem free!
Faint, swim, feist, frisk, feel.
Free-fall
To freer-fall
In finesse unheard.
Is it there
Or is it not there?
Do all these reflected lights
Go through
Or on
This film, this trompe-l'oeil?
Tons
Of thick glass (though falling), metal, concrete,
And, do I see Ariel?

To M.O.M.A.*

Stay, M.O.M.A. and your dream . . .
You flash-light across
The dark corners of my mind;
We love beauty, both!
I forget
    the hardness of your cash,
Your noise and the crowds.
I only remember your happy
    happy Cézannes,
Your starkly
    green de Chiricos,
Your regions of colours and secrets,
Redon, Rousseau, Rouault . . .
But, believe me, I shall never
    drown among your Water Lilies
Saved by the Purists
    in the room next door.

* *M.O.M.A. sounds delightfully more like a fertility goddess than the abbreviated Museum of Modern Art (New York). As I approached the building one windy morning, multi-coloured banners flapped wildly each bearing M, O, M, A; and I heard the advance of MOMA, MOMA, MOMA, MOMA, accompanied with drums.*

Mountain of Wisdom

The scholars went up the hill like many ants,
The students went up the hill like more ants,
The Officials
Drove up or were driven like bigger ants.
All nibbled into the hills
For grains of intellect.
They slice and cut
To renovate the mountain.
They erect concrete towers
To edify the Hong Kong citizenry,
To impress their American friends.
This new edifice
Culls from nature
Its greatest genius:
Wisdom from wild winds,
Knowledge from the drenching rain.
Across the waters, Ma-On-Shan
Boasts of neither art nor artifice.
Its sleek lines
Rise to peaks
Then drop to valleys
With less labour
Than the parabolic curve.
And ants crawl liberally there, without degrees.

Cherry Tree Wood

Young in a soft resilience,
Cherry tree makes smooth surfaces
And excellent blocks for prints.
The fine grain
Of infinitely small fibres
Makes sinewy response
To the cutter's edge.
It is neither the defeat
Of pliancy nor the inevitable
Breakage of things brittle,
But a willing surrender to the unrelenting,
To the cold of steel
In a rhythm of movement.
Those nerves that cannot escape
The most airy of contacts,
Shrivel and die
At knife's shock.

Wholesome wood,
How you are gouged
Out of all proportions!
Ah, you have been inflicted
With the human touch.

A Confession

She has no part in the lot of mankind.
But finding herself in the lot of mankind.
She feels the need for many friends,
Many people, many husbands,
Many fathers, many mothers.
Her children are many vanities
She uses to batter her husbands,
Her parents and her people with.
These that have nothing to do with her,
Except for her many vanities.

O God, When Do You Find Me Guilty?

Those who are vain, I am more vain;
Those who lie, I can lie better.
I would if I could manipulate
Others and their lives to suit my better purposes.
I would deny you when you are inconvenient;
But in fear pray to you.
Yet when do you find me guilty
When I can find none guilty?
I fear the murderer, the knifer, the raper;
But I don't know
The man who murders, knives or rapes.
I hate the mother who hates me a daughter;
But I don't know the woman who was child then wife.
Do you condemn me because you know?

Underdeveloped

I make of my poems
A cushion for my tired head,
For I have known fear
From my mother's hands.
My mind sickened
By milk from her breasts
I now twirl my tongue
Round mammalian taste.
Like puppies
Licking their lips
After a drink of milk.
But puppies are nice
With their paws and their tails
While I sense my height and my years.

I Hold My Past

I hold my past in the cup of my own hands.
– A large collection of images,
Of many places and many smells,
Some more painful than others.
Colours brilliant or drab,
Events that show the condition inhuman –
These do not make a picture.
The images, scattered by constant change,
    are not connected.
What lurks in the hollows
Between time and time?
An absence of adhesion,
Like mother's love, perhaps.
The eternal spaces and
The eternal child, both ignorant.
How little that amounts to,
The cup of one's own hands.

Excreta Tauri
(Intone the Title and Read the Rest at a Run)

the moment of knowing
like all moments
is as unique as general
for we all know
something or other
at some time or another
though the niceness of a particular slant
or the perfect timing of a split second
goes to show that what I know
is never as you know it
when you know it
in any case
those in the know
will tell you
they know they'll never know
and so
knowing the absolute democracy of none and never to know
is all you and I will ever know

Poetry Is Never of Emotion

Poetry is never of emotion.
It is a compromise
Between what the soul desires
And what the flesh cannot give.
For the healthy man
His life is his poem.
For the literary critic
He lives to write another article.
It is the poet
Who shuffles from kitchen to loo
Biting his nails not knowing what to do.

The Sculpted Hand

The arm bent upwards,
Sticking from beneath the quilt,
Ends with the hand.
The hand, erect, fixed
In time and space,
Holding cigarette, drifting smoke.
The power of being still, hand cold, erect:
Holding space and time.
What has that hand to do with the dry throat?

Raw

Raw as an open wound that insists
On the extremity of pain
In order to reach fulfilment
Is every desire.
But pain is only secondary
To that need
Of exploitation
To a fullness which
Cuts and then numbs.

When Tired and Sleepy

Resolve
Never again
To shake father's meagre frame
Or blame mother's small heart.

Night's acid bites.
It smoothes lines, angles, contours,
All unique features.
Darkness is a strong colour,
It dyes all
And changes
All into large patterns, immense forms,
Too large, too large for hate alone.

I do not like this night.

Soliloquy of Light

My life, like unto the wick of the candle, is bent and
    gnarled.
Crippled and spent, the life, in me, that was once
Is naught.
Dried and charred, it rests
On the little wax, that will remain
As it is, lifeless.
It will forever
Be
As it is
Holding the wick
Unburning.

Remonstrance and Reply

What vagaries of youth have led to
This indulgence in black and white?
This tonal gradation within one colour
Is just so limiting!
Child, iron out your rancour
And let it hang in the sun.

Mothers of hate
Roots of woe
Sons born in hate hating grow.
Born and bred in the dark
I only hope to become
As fair as any prize potato.

Notes before Bedtime

Who killed my mother's joie de vivre?
Was it the nuns?
Was it the nuns?

Was it the nuns who
Tossing in their beds at night
Blame the heat
When they can't sleep?

———

Short termed excitement
At having a poem printed
Or having finished a paper
Feels false, proves false.
The discomfort of excitement
Overflowing this present cup.

Letter to My Brother

Home is depressing to-day
Because of remnants from yesterday.
We hang scrolls
To hide cracks on the walls;
We put father's vases all in a row
To collect water from the leaking roof.
By the light of a naked bulb
We stare through curtainless windows
At tall bamboos swaying and rustling
Etched against a dark still sky.
And I remembered when as children
We entertained each other
At night in the summer house
With our servants at our beck and call.

Miniature Trees

The idea, I think, is to squeeze
The life from an aged plant
And rejuvenate it in miniature.
Not to preserve the dregs of age
But to use the iron rigour of a stump
To sustain life in young shoots
That live to adorn man's will,
While human hands train, twist, slit or break them.

Firstly choose from nature,
(Slave market of abundance)
The right tree for your purpose,
One shaped with potential beauty.
Plant it in your garden and see that it lives.
Then pluck its soul,
Trim its roots, its shoots later.
It must not die
But grow to the size and shape you desire
In your porcelain dish.
In years to come, subjugated nature will respond to
    your vigilance.

The straight pine sapling
Straining its young neck to the sun
Can be made in time to frown authority
As it cuts downwards in angles, twists and turns.
The rugged black miniature elm
At last, sprouting young green branches and small leaves
Takes on eminence in its ancient fertility.

On the Double

"I must, then, stretch myself
Across 24 years, in 24 hours.
Though tissues and nerves, there are not enough
For pain to turn into pleasure:
The wrong timing of the wheel numbs too quickly,
Too great a length breaks the body too soon".
In concentrated violence, the taut body explodes,
Rocking the rack till it no longer holds.

Of Strawberries (From D. to A.)

"Your breast in my hand
Is firm, shaped, smooth,
Yet entirely soft and supple.
Light as dew,
Clear as a starry night,
With so much in so little.
So small, inside my hand
Your breast
Like a strawberry, full of
Mystery, holding globules of moisture
In thin tissues of sweetness and life.
I touch your nipple
I hold you tight
I kiss you
And know
That after all
Your breast is not a strawberry."

Local Habitation 1994

"... the poet's pen
Turns them to shapes, and gives to airy nothing
A local habitation and a name."

— Shakespeare

"Lutte avec le carrare,
Avec le paros dur . . ."

— Théophile Gautier

What's in a Name

I whispered it
I insinuated it
I referred to it
only as acronym.
For it rhymed too well
with ting tong sing song
King Kong and ping pong.
In any case
it sounded
hardly like it should.
That was twenty years and more.
These days the name
sits comfortably
on the lips of politicians
and the fashionable alike.
You can be sure
a name comes of age
when others use it as metaphor.
In the U.S.
boomtown Miami
is now called
the Hong Kong of the Americas.

Hong Kong at the Crossroads

The city has become.
adjunct to its airport.
The airport has become
a mere coach station
for families strung out
across oceans and continents.
"The family at home"
used to refer to one place at a time.
It will now be redefined.

Towards University Station

To the left a painted scene,
almost like a Scottish loch at dusk,
blue grey blue silver,
monochrome.
To the right thick-set banana groves,
intense luxuriance,
close enough
to hold the secret
of Jalil Ibrahim's body,
murdered for opposing new loans for CARRIAN.
Then the towers of the university
begin to rise hugging the hills.
A big loop round the headland,
and the train stops here.

The Carrian Group is at the heart of a long drawn-out complex financial fraud case.

Home to Hong Kong

A Chinese
Invited an Irishman
To a Japanese meal
By the Spanish Steps
In the middle of Rome
Having come from Boston
On the way home

Canticle on a Drop of Water

Like a drop of water the will
Hovers above without contact
Adjacent to but always detached from
Its limbeck which is the soul
The will keeps distance
It flows free
Of any agent
Sufficient that it is itself
At all times
In all places

31

Mai Po, 1990. Illustration by Louise Ho.

Living on the Edge of Mai Po Nature Reserve

This garden this stream these marshes,
A bird sanctuary among mangroves,
Herons perch egrets glide,
The hills gather from afar.

On a clear day
To the left to the right
Rise shadows of city blocks,
The other side of Hong Kong, Shenzhen, China.

At night, a long row of lights like jewels,
Marks the electrified high fence
From one end to the other.
Our Berlin Wall, looking innocuous,
Bathed in the warm glow of the Chinese city.

The horizon closes in like two long arms.
We are surrounded,
China holds us in an immense embrace.
Merely the lie of the land.

Hong Kong Riots II

Stand your ground
even if for only
two foot square.
The sentry's box
the railings
the imposing gate posts
were plastered
with posters.
People stood
upon others' shoulders
plastering posters
outside
the Governor's house.
Many months
and nothing broke through
the marching
the chanting
the burning
the bombs.
The stiff upper lip
held tight.
The anti-riot police
grouped
like so many Roman turtles
stood their ground.
Rain or shine
surrounded by crowds

outside
the Governor's house
the sentry stood
khaki shorts
rifle in hand
still as a statue
and held his ground
of two foot square.
This too is pomp and circumstance
without fanfare.

"Cloud Gate Dance Theatre":
Three Dances

I

He bent the air like a reed
greenly loined and a green dash
over his chest
Nijinsky's Faun
could have danced this way
he landed like a sliding leaf
silently on the balls of his feet

He flies like a bird
he hugs the floor like a frog
he leaps like a springbok
he sweeps the stage like an elf

Elfin perfect elfin bright
flesh made elfin elfin light

II

Never a cloud god so muscularly shown
dancing at cloud level throughout
hoisted up high
on the shoulders of two others
half dancers half shadows dressed in black
he wears the mask of the god of thunder
his many muscles bulge like so much cumulus
he circumnavigates the stage
like so many clouds

III

They fell they splintered they exploded
like Chinese New Year fire crackers
to the sound of fire crackers

Then their gestures changed
they jerked and grimaced
before they fell
to the sound of bullets
then a hail of bullets
and complex variations of falling

Then the lights of a tank shone
straight at the audience
one man stood firm
then he jerked and fell

Remembering 4th June, 1989

Yes, I remember Marvell, Dryden,
Yeats, men who had taken up the pen
While others the sword
To record the events of the sword
That would have vanished
Were it not for the words
That shaped them and kept them.

The shadows of June the fourth
Are the shadows of a gesture,
They say, but how shall you and I
Name them, one by one?
There were so many,
Crushed, shot, taken, all overwhelmed,
Cut down without a finished thought or cry.

Presumably, that night, or was it dawn,
The moon shone pure,
As on the ground below
Flowed the blood of men, women and children.
The stunned world responded, and
Pointing an accusing finger, felt cheated.

But think, my friend, think: China never
Promised a tea party, or cakes
For the masses. It is we,
Who, riding on the crest of a long hope,
Became euphoric, and forgot
The rock bottom of a totalitarian state.

Then, this compact commercial enclave,
First time ever, rose up as one.
Before we went our separate ways again,
We thought as one,
We spoke as one,
We too have changed, if "not utterly"
And something beautiful was born.

As we near the end of an era
We have at last
Become ourselves.
The catalyst
Was our neighbour's blood.

Whoever would not
For a carefree moment
Rejoice at a return
To the Motherland?
But, rather pick ears of corn
In a foreign field
Than plough the home ground
Under an oppressive yoke.

Ours is a unique genius,
Learning how to side-step all odds
Or to survive them.
We have lived
By understanding
Each in his own way
The tautness of the rope
Underfoot.

Like Pilgrims

Like pilgrims we have come
from far and near
in the name of inter-
nation-alism
We have come to learn
how to break barriers
how to enlarge our visions
we have also come
to lay the turf
on the recent past.

Graz, old city, Roman settlement.
Throughout the ages
a city marked by history.
We were told
of Turkish invasions
of the Counter Reformation
and other items of other worlds
framed in gold and Baroque.

We were told
of the bombings
how the city
was nearly flattened
during the war.

Let us hold our peace
let us keep
the silence of
the Anschluss
the goose step
the flowing banners
of red and black.

At the invitation
of the city
for one of its regular
arts festivals
Hans Haacke
built in 1988
a replica
of the 1938
wooden column
which circled
the soaring obelisk
in the town centre.

The first column
was erected
to celebrate
Hitler's Victory Marches.

Haacke's column
repeated the same
plus copies of documents
of the Anschluss attached.

One peaceful Sunday morning
Haacke's column
was fire-bombed.
That same year
Mr. Kurt Waldheim
was elected
President of Austria.

Friends, tread gently
for you tread
on the dead.
Let us tend the grass
grow flowers
lest we be bombed again.

Jamming

"A great while ago the world begun"

                                        geeleegulu

An oaf pretending to things intellectual
Stamping and stammering pronounced
"Beauty
Is in the eye
Of the beholder"

                                        geeleegulu

The editor crossed out Menteth
To put in Macbeth, carelessness
Or plain be-loo-dy ignorance

                                        geeleegulu

"Ooooh, do you think
She can tell the difference
Between irony and mere cliché"
"Ah, you have lived here too long
Deafened by the intricate cacophonies
Of our urban mill
You now guess at speech
By looking at the face of the speaker"

                                        geeleegulu

He wants "to be married"
China Bride wants out of the country
She has minimal English
He has minimal Chinese
Between them it can only be

                                        geeleegulu

Have you ever tried merging
The time-stressed with the syllable-stressed
Within one discourse

                        geeleegulu

Call it what you will
Variously-tongued
Multicultural
Cosmopolitan or apartheid
Each is to the other

                        geeleegulu

Bacon didn't trust it much
But Churchill thought it rather grand
On these our very own shores
Let us make our very own

                        geeleegulu

Die speech die language
Words have lost their currency
The world is too old and
There is nothing more to say

                        geeleegulu

Geeleegulu is a Cantonese colloquial onomatopoeic reference to English as "Double Dutch".

First Stop: Frankfurt

Fractured vision
kaleidoscopic
Cubist perspectives
cut the al fresco café.
Between waking and sleeping
the eye catches
the split planes of cups and plates.
Fifteen hours away
lay Hong Kong.
Two minutes away
lay street sleepers
some on mattresses
under bridges
some behind tin hovels
complete with hanging geranium.

Vase

Indifferent colours half defined
Water-lilies largely submerged
Straining for clarity
Discontented with half-knowledge

Thin net-work of capillaries
Course down opalescent glaze
Seeking the biscuit bed
Cutting into the heart of things

City

No fingers claw at the bronze gauze
Of a Hong Kong December dusk,
Only a maze of criss-crossing feet
That enmeshes the city
In a merciless grid.

Between many lanes
Of traffic, the street-sleeper
Carves out his island home.
Or under the thundering fly-over,
Another makes his own peace of mind.

Under the staircase,
By the public lavatory,
A man entirely unto himself
Lifts his hand
And opens his palm.
His digits
Do not rend the air,
They merely touch
As pain does, effortlessly.

The Blind Samurai

After the violence the noise
The split-second multiple kill
The quick sortie
The cunning strategy
The chivalrous run
The Blind Samurai always went to the sea
Cross-legged he sat and listened
Attended to the ebb and flow
The waves lapping took him apart
Gradually to a world apart
He breathed with them
He felt them come over him
He became the waves

They restored the order
By which he saw
Became his light

When his sword
Circumscribing his world
Prescribed life and death

In the Warm Glow

In the warm glow
of a Devon late afternoon
Ina and I lay stretched out
on the grassy slope
arms splayed
our bodies against the earth
hugging it

In the dusty afternoon
of a Hong Kong winter drought
a young man lay stretched out
on the asphalt of a busy street
arms extended
his body against the ground
inert dead
having just jumped down
he loved the earth
too much
too soon

Polite Conversation

The winnowed sun in a shade of green
Cradles the crispy English tongue
In the spring.
My sun at home
Is a scourge,
Searing the brain to submission.
But neither
Is like yours,
Ringing of ancient rites
And mysteries untold,
Gaunt pale people
From the North.
You (with your Nordic limning,
Like a medieval Christ)
Find this place, you say,
Short of primary colours,
Clear definitions,
That England has played her games for too long,
Become suave and is dying.
I confess to liking her latitudes,
If nothing else.
Your white vestments shimmer in half light,
And you look very tall.

Apple Tree

for how much
to defer
the apple
from the apple tree
distance between
in deference
to you to me
by five minutes

in deference
you to me five minutes by
(so) much to defer
minutes on the tree
how the apple leaves

leaves how much
more in deference
to five minutes

fruit cleaned of tree
no deference left or wanted

A U.K. poet wrote the middle 8 lines, I wrote the first 8 and the last 2.

49

A Bit of Luck

My wife and I were waiting for the bus in Canberra one Saturday afternoon. It was a sunny day in winter and we were on holiday. Soon I noticed that a woman sitting next to us was attempting eye-contact and was on the verge of a smile. The clement weather brings out the sociable in people, I suppose. Beautiful day, I said. It transpired that she managed to buy the handbag she was cuddling at a very low price that morning. It was the only one left, and she was clearly very pleased with herself. The bag was ghastly, faded plastic and lopsided. That was lucky of you, put in my wife trying to say something nice. She smiled, drew on her cigarette and said, one always needs a bit of luck in this world.

Mildly eccentric. But that wasn't it, there was something inexplicable about her. She was clearly older than she seemed, she also had a battered look about her, also there was an underlying bubbliness which was almost manic. She chatted on merrily in her very German voice occasionally flattened by the Australian vowel. At one point her sleeve fell back and there was a number etched on her forearm. We tried not to react. She smiled and explained that she was Aryan, not Jewish, she was thrown into the camps because she was a communist, but she managed to escape and came to Australia as a refugee. That was a long time ago, a long time ago, she said, reassuringly.

Image

slice the cliff
in miniature
do not give
the crow
a single foothold
slick as marble
let the black
slide torrential sway
shear down
all sides

Jade

The colour of emerald,
without dark spots and fractures.
Not a crystal,
it has no facets.
Green viscosities
linger in ever
deepening shades
of differing greens.
The atoms move
from stone
to a liquid drop
in space.
Light alone
sets it
in perspective.

Clip Clop

Clip. It was that time of year when humidity hangs visible. Mid-August brings either torrential devastating rains or the scourge of Helios wrapped in static air. Clop. But it was that time of day and in that kind of area where vegetation bathed in half light smells fresh and even the height of summer becomes pleasantly livable. Clip. It was five o'clock in the morning and we were driving down the gently winding gently undulating trunk road past Water Tower University. Clip clop. The plane had been delayed three times from eight o'clock that evening and was due to take off at last at seven o'clock that morning. Clip clop. We had the road to ourselves.

Clip clop, clip clop, clipclop, clipclop. The sound of horse's hooves ringing on macadam became clearly audible and began weaving a complex pattern. It steadily increased as if approaching. The pace was perfectly even, perfectly regular, one complex activity of steady progression. Then it came into sight. One solitary horse, rich chestnut brown, muscles gleaming, was coming towards us in a mechanically steady trot, meticulously following the white line in the middle of the road, oblivious of us, or of anything. It followed the white line as it came out of the bend, it followed the white line as we passed each other, it followed the white line past us, never deviating, never changing its pace.

The intricate sound pattern began to fade in stages into the distance and then was heard no more. Unharnessed. Cameoed.

Tombed-In

textured blindness
of sculpted feel
weight of boulders
surfaces of boulders
that skinned knuckles have battered
foetus of a dying mother
thrashing about for air
a giant
locked in a little box
landbound
tombed in
and nothing opened
not even
not even
by following
the long gaze
of aquamarine

Colours of Corot

Colours of Corot
Assemblage of spirited waste
Cross the unessential waters
Over the transgressive stream

Come into my country of contraries
Learn my digressive tongue
My intensities to coerce
By failure exorcised

Consider the Peppercorn

Consider the peppercorn
Not as doctrine
But as fact
One thing
In exchange for another
Regression from contract
To original barter
My trust (which I have given)
For forgiveness
I would have struck
The better bargain

This is a quibble on the concept of consideration in contract law.

Things Pentecostal

I

the descent
of a floating charge
which seizes on
specific property
upon crystallization
is for some
Pentecostal

II

when the proprieties of success
speaking a social tongue
will have become silent
great minds abashed
by the greater pressures
of trivia
will for a moment
have crossed the cliff-
edge of enlightenment

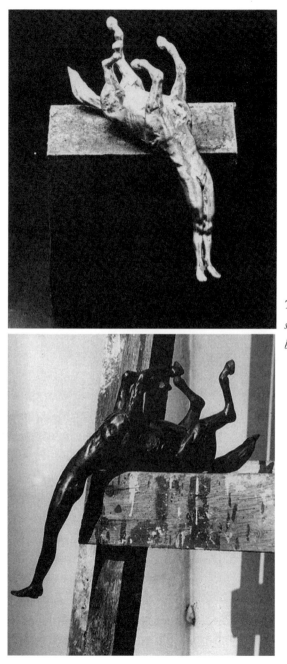

Two views of the sculpture, Bronze Horse, *by Mak Hin Yeung.*

Bronze Horse

Earth is kind
to fall of sparrow
fall of horse.
Iron ore,
ungiving,
props up
sculpted bronze horse
as it breaks its back
on iron pedestal,
its legs
flaying the air.

Tree trunk neck
sprouts athlete's legs.
Taut thighs
direct downwards
where horse's head
would have arched upwards.
Two motions clash
like trains
into each other's velocity,
two bodies
countermining,
two contraries
forced into one orbit:
the unseen body,
fully in control,
meets the unseen head,
losing control,
at the neck
of a bronze horse.

Mother Has Just Turned Seventy

Mother has just turned seventy, but her hair has gone white a long time ago. There she stands, her shock of white hair blending in its outer edges with the light of the sun, together they shine like a halo. Her white tunic gleams down the middle where her bright green mantle parts at the front. It looks more like an ecclesiastical cope than a mantle. It drapes, it falls into place, it flows, it plies and bends with the movements of her body, it sweeps the grass, then it sweeps her body. She continues on her way, effortlessly, lightly, as if the cape grows from her very body. She is one with this magnificent green that seems to shine with an inner light, that seems to glisten like rows and rows of tiny sequins and yet its edges glide over the grass as naturally as if it belongs there.

The light from behind her head prevents me from seeing her face clearly. It seems transfused with light. I crouch into the grass, as if mesmerized. She keeps approaching where I am without seeming to get very much closer.

Ah yes, she does come closer now, at long last. Now I begin to see her face clearly.

Her black eyes penetrated or so I felt. I breathed a sigh of relief. My body sagged, almost sobbing, into a state of complete and utter abandon. It felt like coming home.

Ten minutes ago, still crouching in the grass, I felt a sharp piercing bite. I started in pain. I then saw a bright green bamboo snake winding its way in big loops over the grass, its scales shimmering in the sun. The green bamboo snake is registered as one of the most venomous snakes in the land. Help is out of the question. This is the wilderness and there is no one within reach.

Black Hole

There is a black hole at the back of my head that stretches into infinity. It is always there, blatantly or latently. It is there during my waking hours, whether I'm walking or sitting down, working or idling. It is sometimes felt as a lump inside me, sometimes in the throat. Sometimes it causes contraction in the chest, then, I would have to inhale deeply in an attempt to relieve the difficult breathing and to send the choking feeling as far as possible back to where it belongs. That is, I suppose, referred sensation, not unlike referred pain.

On wintry days I would see it at a great distance, especially when I close my eyes. As I begin to get used to the dark, it starts to grow, slowly, bigger and bigger, until it gets so big, I find myself in it.

It has a tremendous force. Anything within a certain periphery is lost to its firm, steady, inexorable pull. It enfolds you and you become nothing. All my life, in varying degrees, I've had to fight off that force. Constantly afraid that it would swallow me up, I keep my eyes bulgingly open, on the qui vive all the time. When I reach exhaustion, I drop off for a moment, only to wake up with a start and a jerk, fearing for my life.

Fragment

as the moment of sense loosens
parts of meaning fall slightly out of step
but do not signify nonsense
being only sense out of time

Well-spoken Cantonese

How praise the beauties of a gracious man
Except that they are the graces of a beautiful man?
Tone, stress, diction, timing, all combine
To make the texture of his voice:
So rare anywhere
But rarest of all, here.
His modulated resonance
Creates a civilized space
Or a proper silence,
Which was not there
Before he spoke.

Soliloquy of a White Jade Brooch

I was pretty
She loved my prettiness
Discarded me

I was discarded
By a child of seven
Because she loved me

She discarded me
For the other
Complex design

Intricate carvings
Cold geometry
A shrine and a monk within

My large round butterfly wings
She loved. She loved
My white viscosities

What voice in her
Made her choose
Only the unpleasurable

Hemmed in by
Strictures
She'll probably
Have to learn
How to live
For the rest
Of her pretty little life

After Yeats

I saw her gliding down the corridor,
Her chin tilted at a small angle,
Her eyes in a distant gaze.
I had thought that face
A fitting subject for any fine brush.

Memory then yielded another head,
With chin slightly tilted,
A face flanked by yellow braids,
Her eyes held in the distance.
Botticelli's mistress, sister
Of Amerigo Vespuci,
(The latter gave one country its name),
Venus, Primevera, Virgin Mary and others,
To adorn a wall or a ceiling,
In those vibrant days of bright clarity.

I know her now; and though of
Polish-German stock, an American.
Is she her parents' child
Or Venus's double?
Which of her forms has shown her substance right?
Gyres run on.
But that face, that face
Will always be Botticellean.

Acrostics

In the morning
I felt the weight of centuries.

Centripetal
Force of the insane,
Only aware
Of awareness itself.
Tension enough
To hold time,
As if with one hand
To stop
A rolling tank.
They that leap boundaries
Have committed a personal sin,
Pain's due is an individual's privilege.

How far away have I to go
That it may leave me?
To retire to what scarcity
So as to be rid of it?
Will the rain soften this lengthy pain
If I give it another minute?

Last night, I saw you from afar,
I foundered and lost my way.
I failed to reach you,
Barred by my own acrostics.
I felt the weight of centuries.

A rolling tank: what was meant a bizarre image in 1983 became nightmare reality in 1989.

Slow Rain

slow rain from a slow sky
falling on a slow pulse
grinds each moment to a halt
each step a numbing footfall
on uncertain ground
eyes looking inwards
lose their focus

is this a time of waiting
of abnegation of blindness
for a grief turned inwards

severance is not all
it leads to change
a shifting of sand underfoot

dull thudding of heart and head
like distant hooves
and the clattering
of steel on stone
all through the night

Apprehension of Beauty

Apprehension of beauty is pain. It is in the nature of beauty to hurt when apprehended. I loved your beauty, noted your rare grace and was hurt by both.

In my own timing, in my own way, I have come into my own through celebration of another's existence.

Born Catholic, heathen at heart, how shall I explain my pagan intensities to your Christian God?

For Foone, Brighton 1978

You that claim
To live by water, air, sun, love and poetry,
You hold existence in your palm
Like a trapped bird,
And when you set it free,
You glory in the flight
That launches you both.

Discipline

Ghost-glide above surfaces
Float gentle over ground
Soft-drift down stream and heather
Touch is harsh
The vacant and the void

I reached for the one way I knew
The straight-jacket's veto
But loosen the organs of sorrow
For sorrow cutting on sorrow
Will help to blunt its edge
Such are our passions
When the intelligence touches the heart

The outward shape
For the inner desire
Expression exactly conveyed
The will at one with body
Conscience and instinct
Having at last merged
We grow towards
The quality
Of being fine

The Cold Keeps Me Out

The cold keeps me out
Stings me and keeps me out
With my animal warmth
I am fenced off
Driven back
By the cleanliness
Of finer things
They that
Look better
Untarnished

Russet autumn
Set within air
Arrested by cold
Nevertheless grows
In its own coldness
Ferns unfurl
Among endless
Fronds of green life
Drop of water
Glistening
Locked
Like a diamond
Is cold

A Burning Inadequacy

a burning inadequacy
scours the heart
to submission
rock-hewn intents
dissolve eventually
into water
a passionate vagueness
directs to another place
another time

The Hind-wheel of a Double-decker Bus

The hind-wheel of a double-decker bus wound in a body, squashed it for a quarter of a mile before the driver knew what had happened and stopped. Later, the Medical and Health Department had to go back on that quarter mile to pick up the flattened bits. This sort of thing doesn't happen very often. Normally, people only get dragged along because the driver doesn't stop long enough for passengers to get off. Sometimes, heads get a bit fractured or a little broken, at other times, limbs get trapped or truncated, fingers get subtracted perhaps, but people don't die that easily.

No Swan

Gargantuan pelican mouthing the void
to catch the last drop of bliss
her thighs coagulate.
Vault tumbling on vault,
wave after wave,
at length lengthily,
his soul gave out.
Impress of swan-like caress
on smooth skin
of young Hakka girl
gave no sacred sign,
only the weight
of a man
with a touch of diabetes
and fifty plus winters
on his sagging jowls

Prayer

Thirty days O Lord
of faithful concentration
to find out Your will
and I do believe
with all conviction
my soul can muster
my duty lies with Lucinda
please Lord confirm for me
my erstwhile vow
to serve You compels me
to serve You according
to the prompting
of my soul
that my heart waking
at a late hour has
finally found the truth
in the acute bond
that must combine her soul
with mine to Your greater glory

The bell for lectures went
for one moment he cursed
Rome's silence
Good God he said
as he rushed out of his office
why can't I do what everybody else does

The Long Frown

the apex looming high
above the nose
and between the eyes
firmly rooted
on the brow
it projects
two limbs down
flanking first
the nose
then the mouth
an Eiffel Tower
for a face
one so young
and pretty too

her husband
tall and lanky
certainly "carbuncular"
sometimes "pustulate"
though no longer "young"
walks haltingly
having to concentrate on
one
two
and three
hard squints
before taking
one step

Prussian generations ago
they believe in marching
in marching always
even when fearful angels fly

What Mother Taught Me

I spent the first seven years of my life trying very hard to learn how not to live. For I have heard mother say that it was better to be dead than to be alive. I did not know then that it was only a manner of speaking, that it was her way of controlling others. I tried everything and failed. I tried anorexia nervosa, I tried insomnia, I tried constipation, I tried all sorts of illness and was sometimes hospitalized, but failed to stop myself from being alive. Then from aged seven onwards I learnt how not to live even with staying alive. Now this was easier. I became so good at it I could slip in and out of non-living very easily. The stasis of non-living is beyond time, beyond wear and tear, beyond means and meaning.

Three Men in a Lift, Not to Mention the Woman Who Didn't Get In

It was a University function held at the Art's Centre on the Island. The Arts Centre is a fifteen-minute walk away from the city centre, what the locals call prime-land. This was for some years the most costly piece of land in the world, it is now the third most costly, after Tokyo and London. The city, represented by the Urban Council, had been hankering after such a centre for decades, neither private nor public sector paid any attention, the arts being hardly a lucrative activity. It was finally built because some clever bureaucrat detected an angle of space in between two high-rise buildings which could be made into a triangle. At least it would be a variation on going round and round in circles. It is aesthetically interesting too, it's like fitting a neat compact triangular Pompidou Centre of a box in between the legs of a sleeping giant. And so the New University had seen fit to mix and mingle with the suave urbanites in their environment instead of holding the reception out in the wilds of the country-side campus.

Guests and university personnel alike were arriving in hordes, jamming the triangular lobby, waiting to take the lifts that would take them to higher triangles. Men in dark suits, women dripping in jewels and finery jostled about elbowing their way everywhere. This was twenty-first century civilization where a dissociation of finery from fine manners had firmly set in.

Bringing up the rear, about a lift-load away, was a group of four trying to make conversation and visibly straining. I was later to learn that the three men were high-ranking administrators in a university run by administrators and the woman only an academic, and a junior one to boot. The unspoken rationale was that any academic who rose high enough in the ranks would become administrator. Indeed, the administration was the university. Academics were incidental additions as somehow courses had to be offered and students somehow had to be taught. The young-looking man on the left was Petronius Ong, recently Harvard Phd'd and positively glowing, now dean of students in one of the colleges. The one on the right was Aloysius Jing, son of pre-communist Chinese Mandarin, American educated, just returned from Cambridge, U.K., full of praise for "the civilised manners of the English". The man in the middle was T.S. Tan, president of one of the colleges, who refers to Lord Todd by his first name, etc., etc.

The lift arrived. People got out. People got in. As the four neared the lift entrance, it became clear there was only room for three. As if caught in mid-sentence, for a split second facial muscles tensed up and the four shared a blank look. No one actually made a mad dash, they just straightened their backs and looked vague.

Then everything happened very quickly. The three men moved towards the lift and just as they did so, the woman took one big deliberate step backwards. It was at this point that she caught my eye and we burst out laughing together.

She came up to me as I leant against the counter and explained that that was perhaps the refugee spirit which was so infectious in this colony. Three presumably civilized men couldn't resist getting into a lift as if it was the last lift available, the last meal, the last boat, the last chance. You're a journalist, she called to me as she was about to board an empty lift, write about it, make someone laugh!

There was a last gesture that struck me as interesting. I wonder if she noticed, perhaps women don't. That tableau of the lift doors about to close, the three men were standing in a straight line, all three of them held their hands together in front of their trousers, as if protecting themselves. I know, a lot of nonsense has been made of Hitler and his hands-over-his-crotch pose. However, can there really be some truth in man's fear of castration being the basis for all other fears, including the fear of missing out on a lift? I'll be damned if I'm going to find out!

The Passionate Lovers

The passionate lovers
Tore at it as never before.
Smooth round plums
Bursting at the seams,
A whole orchardful of sweetness.
And heaven blessed the day
And made it fruitful.

At last the nine-months' wonder came,
The glory of her loins,
And of mankind, she thought.

Thirty years
And the world wakes up
To find a limp hand
Clutching a limp heart,
Shaking and stuttering,
The worm of a being,
A stranger to himself
And the world,
Unloving and unloved.
Who could have known
So much zest
Went into his making?

A Neighbour's Tale

she was held
in the fullness
of a synthesis
by her conscious mind
while he excelled
in the graces
of the unconscious
every night
she witnessed
her husband
in his guttural snore
drawn to great length
as he breathed in
then the swishing
through the mouth
as he breathed out
making bubbles
before she retired
to her own room
next door

To Grandfather
(Monsieur Emmanuel Allaye Chan)

Rum-pa-pa papaya banana
Ma's papa grandpapa Allaya,
And what were you doing on Beach Pattaya?
At your funeral
I rubbed
My bouquet of white roses
Against beautiful aunt Mary's buttocks
As they drew the figure eight
In the procession.
She turned round,
I looked innocent.
At the village Church in Quatre Bornes,
Your wife arranged for you
A third class service,
There being only servants
And their families.
At the Cathedral in Port Louis
She gave you grand first class rites
With priests coming out
To receive your coffin
With cross and candles.
I was scandalized at the difference,
Being only nine.
Now, I think your wife was being sensible.
Three years before,
Back in Hong Kong,
At great-grand-aunt's birthday banquet,
You tickled aunt Mary,
And her firm round breasts
Baubled to your rhythm,
Also in the figure of eight.

Desire

desire
the static
the unchanging
the permanent
space thus
air still
bowl of water by the window
water unmoving
which does not evaporate
surface of water
smooth
clear
where no grain of dust settles
life that has no echo
matter intensely pure
in a seizure of fixity endlessly

Once upon a Time

Once upon a time there was no human life but a lump, trembling like a festering boil into some sort of life from the fusion of two cells in a mass of bilious, viscous, slimy bilge, among tadpoles and gargoyles, worms and larvae, wriggling things that twisted and turned in a land-locked pool that stank of rotting flesh, diseased foetuses, and dung, a stench that burned through the nostrils and scorched the lungs.

The Awful Belief

the awful belief
through a moment's daring
in the mind's
intrinsic
order
to incise
to incise inextricably
a shape
a firm shape
even in wild sounds
does not say that
what the mind gives
is given
ordered
intrinsically

There Are No Monkeys Here

There are no monkeys here. The Water Tower University is spread over several hill-tops and plenty of greenery, but there are no monkeys. Over the mountains to the south side of Sann Tien, near the reservoir, is a sheltered valley where monkeys live and breed; but that is another place with another story.

On the evening of the fifth of July, something strange took place in the undergrowth near Residence Number Nine on the campus. In the midst of the commotion, a monkey shot out, with blood on its mouth. Then followed the shrieks of a female voice interspersed with the calling of "Jake, Jake" in the most heart-rending desperation.

Jake came to the Department of Commercial Studies three years ago. It was one of those fashionable departments that kept redefining itself. No one in the department knew what it was doing, nor did anyone else in the University. Jake, burly New York Russian Jew, with more than the usual iron in the blood, came, and saw the opportunity amidst the chaos.

He soon became the head of department.

Sometime in the past, he had worked as a bouncer in various night-clubs in New York and Paris. The University did not know about this, but they must have recognised that je ne sais quoi in him, since what they wanted was indeed a bouncer for the department.

As for Jake, it was a good salary, there were additional perks, and the campus provided from time to time diversion in the form of about-to-divorce wives looking for a novel perch, any kind of perch.

One such was Mrs. Brentshaum, the wife of the Professor of Morbid Anatomy in the newly founded and much publicised Medical School. She had been contemplating divorce before she came with her husband. She came anyway because the Far East was exotic. Jake was in the process of divorcing his Catholic wife, but she did not come over with him, even though the Far East was exotic.

Mrs. Brentshaum and Jake made love often and well, to the complete satisfaction of both.

All was going very well until Jake fell in love with a pretty young girl.

The last time he had anything to do with Mrs. Brentshaum was the Christmas of two years ago, when, for reasons unfathomable to the outsider, Jake gave her a monkey for Christmas.

Whatever symbiosis may or may not have grown between animal and mistress is anybody's guess. Occasionally, she was seen carrying the monkey like a nursing child, walking about campus with the animal's arms around her neck or bodice.

After some months, Mrs. Brentshaum left the University and returned to Florida. Nothing was heard of her since.

As for Jake, he continued to show his biceps at departmental meetings, and his other parts to the other at other times.

The pretty young girl was taut as a stallion, at the same time, soft as many bags of down. Apparently, Jake had, in private, expressed great joy in her wonderful breasts. They were firm and shaped to perfection. Above all, he said, they were topped with a pair of the most luscious pink nipples.

On that most deplorable of days, on the fifth of July, alas the day, it all happened then.

After the evening of the fifth of July, the poor girl was left with only one luscious nipple.

Time's Pummelling

Time's pummelling
On life on life on life on life,
The needle has stuck.
Then, time falls out of step,
Leaving life to grow dense,
In pools of corrupt waste.
My nine-months' mother's womb,
With no menstrual issuance,
Blew up with slimy green black bracken,
To grind me out at birth
A deformed lump.

The Unknown Source

the unknown source
a dark mystery
my mother's womb and uterus
and all the way down and out
this is my greatest insecurity
for I could not have lived
wishing mother were never born

Stravinsky's "Oedipus Rex"

instinct leads
sound follows
the score plunges
like a cataract
round upon round
rushing to the last
piercing note
voices soar higher and higher
while chords plunge in the opposite direction
seeking for passion a passion
when they announce Jocasta's death
the messenger's voice
drops two octaves
the chords surge
to wounding pitch
with man lost in between

It's Been Snowing

It's been snowing heavily and streets with cars and other things are completely covered with snow. Funny, snow always (especially at two in the morning) gives a sense of permanence, unchangingness. It arrests time and things stay. Like a flood it covers all and swamps all but unlike a flood it moves nothing and is in itself unmoving. It reminds me of a Japanese sand garden with patterns raked into the sand. It stays for as long as you leave it, then you flatten it and rake up a new pattern. Cars come and make furrows in the snow, these stay until other cars make other furrows.

For Every Mask

For every mask that we take off there is always one more left on — an endless recession of masks, of depths of withdrawal. As long as there is life, there is the ability to recede further. The self is infinitely reductive and is never reduced to nothing. Alternatively, one can reach out and touch infinitely into the other person, the other thing, the outside, and having always to reach yet further.

Unschooled

Unschooled in human relationships, all passions are registered by their intensities alone. The elation of love towards a woman, a man, a chair, or a dog amounts to the same velocity and the resulting excitement will dissipate in the same way.

I Love the Child in Me

I love the child in me
that I am, that grew, cradled
in me becoming.
The child, then, that was
took a long while
inside the body that I am.
Thirty years, and birth
was almost on the way,
the birth of the child
in me that I was.
Gestation took decades.
In the end
it nearly killed me.

Soliloquy of a Madman

I inhabit
the tunnel world
of twilight
hovering between
sense and sensuality
the tunnel I traverse
is rainbow coloured
cognition pervades like scent
sensation rumbles like earthquake

above ground
you tread your sane steps
in the sun
but you too respond
to the tremor
of the earth
it carries the beat of your heart

New Ends, Old Beginnings 1997

"I was born very young into times that were
very old"

— Eric Satie

". . . a poet's lie
Is multilingual"

— Tadeusz Róewicz

Migratory

You want space
You've got space
Now what do you do with it

I floated alone in my king-size bed
I steered between abysses
To my left 1997
To my right 1788
I hugged the shorelines
Crossed the high seas
And drifted here
Landing on terra firma
Terra Australis

A part of ancient Gondwanaland
Its unique flora and fauna are young
Fossils mirror their living counterparts
The hundred million year Wollemi Pine
Will one day propagate in our gardens
The echidna, spikes on a meat slab
Has tunneled through the ages to us
Having walked with dinosaurs

Another Anglophone settlement
Irish, Cockney, North country
Transported cultures
Transformed in two hundred years
Into new shapes new sounds
And endless possibilities
At first the heart longs
For the absent familiar

Cosmopolitan Hong Kong
Its chaos, its anomalies, its power
Or England, my other world
Or some landmark somewhere
A villa by Serlio on the way
To Erbusco, outside Milan
Or family, relatives
In New York, San Francisco
Vancouver, Toronto . . .

Then, like lightning
The shock of the void struck

The neighbours are kind, the dogs are friendly
The land is veritable Eden, the roads are straight
Tender is the meat, tasty is the fruit
It is the loss, the loss
That grips like a vice
That tightens the spine
And the legs go soft
Space-tost, land-lost
I float, I drift, I hover
Cannot settle
Cannot come to stay

Concentrate
Minutely on
This time, this space
Measure the land
Foot by foot
Step by step

These eight acres
Study each weed
Each blade of grass
Follow each flow of air
Sink the ankles
Touch the ground
Walk normally

These are my songlines
Claiming by declaiming
Over my land
O land, walk with me
May the dust settle
Wherever I may stand

Did You Know

Did you know did you know
The birds they chatter and they clatter
They cackle and they squawk
They guffaw and they talk
They squeak and they speak
They whistle and they hiss
The butcher bird ends every song
With a wuff wuff like a dog
The crow's rough death-rattle
And the long cooing of doves

A hawk hovers
A piercing screech and then silence
With talons holding down the prey
Its beak picks at one feather
Tears it off
Then another
And another

On Seeing Promite on the Shelves

Marmite Vegemite Promite
Dolomite sodomite,
Let them precipitate
And you get floccolite.
The first three are edible,
The edibility of the rest
Is questionable.
It all depends
On how you isolate them
Chemically, parts of dolomite
Won't harm you, I'm sure.
As for the rest
I really don't know.
You could start, I suppose.
By psychoanalysing the one
And drying out the other,
Or is it analysing the one
And tying up the other?
Wait a sec, which is the
One, which is the other?
Ah, piss off, what's the point,
You're right, mate, sod'em, mate.

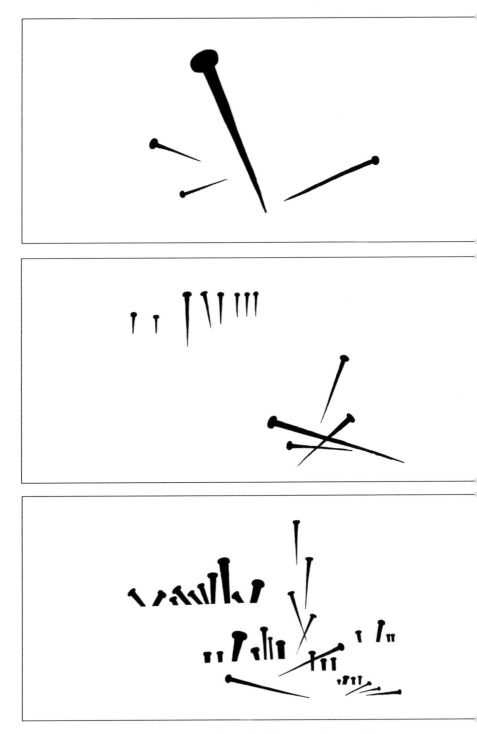

6 Compositions with Nails. Illustrations by Louise Ho.

Conversation

The various declensions
Of layered self-deprecation
The sleight of hand
The tour de force
The quick of an eye
The quarter smile
Positions endlessly qualified
Points developed and redefined
Space made
From artful modesty
The polite insult
Collectively constitute the "whinge" here

January on the Gold Coast

Have I come
To this strange land
Only to be held hostage
By the heat
Every house
Has a fireplace
From open ones
To the most elaborate of boilers
And there is no winter here
Air-conditioning
Is still foreign

And the heat rages from day to day
Confined and confounded
The blank face
Meets the blank day
Surely
Sufferance of suffocating heat
Need no longer be
Part of the human condition

Think you
They are hostage
To their past
Forgetting
They are now in Queensland Australia
Far from some fiercely cold and bleak
English or Irish province
Where heating
Was a hard premium
Sizzle your meats and sausages
On a mightily sizzling day
Heat up your houses
Through the warm winter
Kill the cold
In your ancestors' bones
You live the remains
Of their ancient ravages
Is this the Australian way

Odd Couple

Sleek trim well-groomed
Alert and agile
Walking tall on long legs
Head held high
The other is short and rotund
Waddling on small stumps
Tripping and falling
Trying to catch up
What an odd couple these
An imposing Doberman
And a roly-poly Staffordshire Terrier
They make a team
And are quite harmless really
Until
They encroach
On my cat and its space

Chat

Pretty peroxide blonde
Bright eyes bright smile
Standing on pretty legs and heels
Is always super quick
With her footwork
Sweeping from one wide tangent
To another
In one sentence
Sometimes taking in
The odd non sequitur
And doing well
With the circumstantial metaphor
"He has left his guide dog at the door"
Meaning her carpenter
Botched his job
By not measuring right
Like he was blind

It works
Somewhat like a clever
Three-dimensional
Cockney rhyme

Rambler

Having rambled
Briefly through the UK
Then not so briefly through HK
Though hearing him
You'd think
He never left the parish
He then rambled on
About how the drawers
Didn't fit
The speakers' doors were wrong
The entire cabinet
Was askew
He rambled on
Like a loquacious tinker
You'd never guess
He's in fact a lawyer

By midnight
He was laying down the law
That his teenage son
Was not to sleep
With the girl friend
Under his roof

He has a compass
Keeps his direction
Knows his values
He's a rambler no more

Party

Robotic filings stream down
Shimmering parallel lines
Dusting the estate agent's torso
A Brisbane engineer thinks
Strangely that "Story Bridge" there
Has something to do with English Studies
One "Bob" decided to hold forth
About Shakespeare's "importance"
For being "four hundred years old"
Thus the unschooled small businessman bardologises
The pretty blonde sitting next to him
Slithering in all directions
Among her non sequiturs
Tried progressively to nudge closer
In the course of the evening

The Australian O

No longer pure Cockney
They now mollycoddle it
Melting it in honey and cream
Marinating it in olive oil
From English diphthong to impressive hexaphthong
O for the sensuous Australian O
Rolling through the MTR and around Central
Roll it out
Roll it heaoaium

Knocking at the Door of the Aboriginals

there was a storm
the storm brought
great destruction
and chaos then
out of chaos
came order

history was
history of the tribe
the clan the family
dreaming
was a walking shadow
of yesterday today
tomorrow

civilisations on record
have grown from cities
and the arts of government
Sumerian Egyptian Chinese
African Aztec Mayan Greek
civis civilis civitas

as the settler nation
on this continent of plenty
chews its fingers and toes
trying to eke out
some sort of identity

weave your rich
indigenous culture
into the fabric
of the status quo

decrease the level
of equalizing entropy
locally
and create the genius
of a future age

Coomera Lines

Lines to the spring
Of Coomera
Lines written
At Coomera

Coomera lines
Or is it in a bivouac
At Coomera
I stake out my defence
Against the primitive other

At the Foot of the Mountain

At the foot of the mountain I have a spacious house standing in eight acres of trees and flowers and ponds. A perfect place in which to retire, to recuperate or to die. A place of sustenance, of energy, of growth.

Then, one day, the wind changed. The lowering heavens became white. Out of the corner of my eye I saw the brick walls crumble and fall, the ponds run dry, the trees wither, the lawns turn ashen grey, the soil all desiccated.

Beginnings and Ends

Hard core living is no more than
The body functioning in a continuum
Only remembered by the conscious subject
The rest is act of faith
To make action possible at all
How successfully we deceive ourselves
Into believing there's a significant tomorrow

Storm

First of all the enveloping hot air, ungiving, with not a flicker of movement, a still thermal from which there is no relief. You are surrounded by hot air, buoyed up by hot air, weighed down by hot air. You inhale hot air, you swallow hot air, you feel hot air behind the ears, between the legs, between the toes, under the feet.

Many hours later, a very slight stir, followed by the suggestion of a breeze. The thermal remains.

Yet more hours later, a sudden tearing gust of wind, and the storm has arrived.

Shadows

The shadows lengthen as the days grow short
The complacencies of daylight recede
Dusk demands sharper edges
Etchings and lines in pen and ink
When at last night comes
There are only darker and lighter blotches

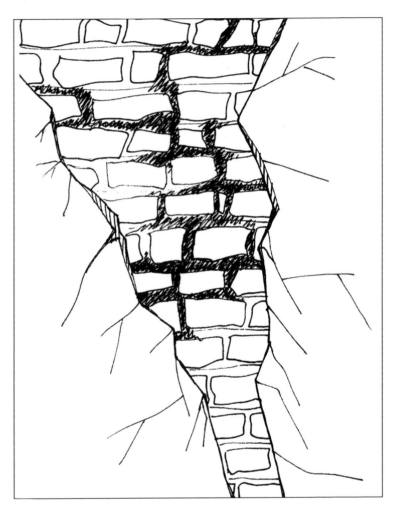

Un-iconic Tree of Life, 1997. Illustration by Louise Ho.

Tree of Life

All torn and twisted shredded and confused
Meandering tree of life a weak pattern
On a brick wall's worn whitish grey grouting
Mere seepage along the way of least resistance
And towards no end in particular
Here's no argument about cause and effect
What happened happened
With little of the wished for or not wished for
Just a breath of air to keep the day alive
Or bones enough to fill some moderate grave somewhere
What matters is context
Affix it just here
This un-iconic pattern
Of a tree of life

End of Era

End of era
Or change of chapter
Smaller than a speck on the map
A nerve centre in the world
Minuscule place
Global space
Several vortices
Suspended by their own velocity
Drive cogwheels that orbit like planets

Walking

I walk against the flow into the crowds, looking into peoples' faces, imploring them to reveal what it is that anchors them. They look so at ease, so contained, so in control. Is it wives, husbands, mortgages, cats, dogs, birds, insects, the sun and stars, or just faith in living? What living? Tiny flats with hardly room for the soul and without universal suffrage. A constantly moving world with receding shorelines which in places suddenly thrust up mountains. Here is mobility with a vengeance, yet people keep their foothold, stay their balance, remain sane.

Island

We are a floating island
Kept afloat by our own energy
We cross date lines
National lines
Class lines
Horizons far and near

We are a floating island
We have no site
Nowhere to land
No domicile

Come July this year
We may begin to hover in situ
May begin to settle
May begin to touch down
We shall be
A city with a country
An international city becoming national

Spirit of Place

Fencit Jarcos Fencit Jarcos
Where have you been
I crossed seven rainbows
Bent the four winds
Seeking the spirit of place
The earth exhaled sounds
Unknown in any language
Shapes unmapped in geometry
Send for new equations
Find a new context
Give it a name
Just follow the drift
In came marching feet clicking heels
Turn
Line upon line of men
Turn
Line upon line of machines
Turn
Line upon line of tanks
Turn
The clock ticked
The moment came

The shock of stasis as nothing happened
The skies didn't turn white
The earth didn't go black
Except in a black and white photograph

FJ what will you do at the end of the day
"I shall spread my wings and fly away"
Stay and follow the spirit of place
"I shall spread wide my wings and go away"
Stay and be my muse
"I shall spread my wings and go far far away"

Flags and Flowers
For N. E. R.

O to be here
Now that the Bauhinia is in bloom
In its mound of purple flowers

They sound the last post
For the last time
At the Cenotaph
Remembering
The eleventh day
Of the eleventh month
And the fields of poppies
For the last time

We too had our fields of red
Flowing beneath
An azure sky
A white sun
It'll be five stars upon red next

Change our flag as you must
But let us keep our speech
Our local voices
Our nine tones
Our complex homophones
Our own configurations of meaning
Our own polite formalities
Our resonances from the Hans of old

Extension I

Dykes and boulders enable
Deep and peripheral structures
To alter the elements
To change natural conditions

(It seems they have to make something entirely new
To see out the old)

Let the offspring swim forth
From inside the cavernous Convention Centre
A whale of an extension
Spouting onto the waterfront
Frozen in glass

Extension II

The figure dips and it sways
It pirouettes then disappears
Behind nooks and crannies
Appearing again in full frontal
It sweeps away
Into a gigantic curve

I follow the flow
Through your bold surfaces
To your most secret interstices
Through your finest mesh
Your exposed girders
I shall remember your multiple nudities
When you become fully dressed
As the largest unsupported space in Asia

A Good Year

Ever an ending that ends so unendingly
Ever a termination so celebrating
1997 is a good year
No better or worse
Than the year before or after

Deadly dead lines kill
They freeze the future
Blocking free passage for the present

The air is lambent with
A collective will to succeed
Almost as if to say
With feet firmly planted on the ground
What matters what flag flies above
We are ourselves to a day

1997 is a good year
As good as any year
It is here

One Hundred Days to Go
For P. Y. W. Lee

The Financial Secretary
Presented his budget recently
We have a surplus
Of three point seven billion dollars

Compound growth
Over the past five years
Was eighty-eight per cent
After inflation

They that are wealthy
Are as always well looked after
They that are wanting
Continue to want

Nineteenth century laissez-faire
Is given a twenty-first century halo
And life goes on
In its unabashed consumerism

Chek Lap Kok

Arid landscape stretching for miles
Over a man-made island
Little men
Little jeeps
Coloured pennants
Criss-cross the dusty yellow earth
From a "Star Wars" movie set
A vast central tower has arisen
Amidst chrome steel fiberglass
And other contorted shapes and sizes

Artifice driven to its limits
Has called for the largest
Urban construction project ever
More costly than the "Chunnel"
It spreads over and under the city
Like a gigantic octopus
Of roads rail bridges tunnels
Train stations grow underground
Above gouged out hollows
The city treads on space

Come to land
In the new airport
In nineteen ninety-eight

Meeting

I met a man yesterday
On the walkway
By the park
We tried to talk
But he spoke a different dialect
He was from the Mainland

He said
That was why
He didn't qualify for welfare
With a withered face and yellowed teeth
Thinking or not thinking
Of the next meal or the next shelter

How dare I
Find value to reside
Only in the works of the human intellect

Hopscotch down the Corridor

Fill the parasitic gaps
With guttural plosives
Grind your aesthetic principles
On the fulcrum of necessity
Measure Li Po's moon
And compare it with Donne's sublunaries
Come and join the fray
Ducdame ducdame

Upon Hearing of a Friend's Death (After Yeats)

Reaching down the dark recesses
Are pictures
Grey skies lowering
Prison walls
Bursting lungs
Stagnant rime
Against all of these
You gave respite
You sheltered me from the screaming heavens
I had thought
Of more formal proferring
Of thanks later
Too late
Now that you've beaten me to the light
Gentle born of gentle clans
One more lost of the so few
Of the "old stock"
I now walk silent among the busy crowds
I cower under their collective might

Discomfort

Disjointed sinews
Twisted guts
The knock at the door
Hovering things in mid-air
Walls and ceilings closing in
My feet walking back to front
Hanging drawing and quartering
Being Pooh Bear full of honey
Stuck inside a hole
Out of all that and more emerges
A structure of meaning in words
Sometimes known as poetry

My Crown Jewels

My crown jewels
Those fat thick lumps
Cradled snugly
Inside my upper jaw
The cysts that grew
Layer upon layer
Decade upon decade
Like pearls they grew
Skin over skin
Until
One fine day
My face blew up
My jewels
Crowning thirty years of cankered waste

Tilting

Professor Pye has a nose cut short
His nostrils are two train tunnels
Which he tilts at you
In great earnestness

A graduate student admirer
Soft and willowy
Rounded and smooth
In conversation
Tilts her pelvis back and forth

Fulcrum at the neck
Fulcrum at the hips
He tilts
She tilts
They tilt

Dr Hero Joh

Joh-y Joh Hero Joh
a hero Hero Joh
what a name to live up to
his father called him so

Here to-day there to-morrow
shunted to and fro
where to ever next he asked
the Faculty'll have me
the Head said so

Cautious Joh did the right thing
thought the right thought
walked the right step
the right people liked him
down the Byzantine way
to the headship
as the old Head's head rolled

Since then
every new head
became displaced replaced
by Hero Joh
Joh Joh-y Hero Joh
called a hero and is so

New Poems

Reflection

Your shade
in the water
Your reflection
in the shade
Tell of the sun's
direction
As it covers
your reclining form

Not being Narcissus
The self does not dissipate

Watch how pool upon pool
The water grows limpid
Under your steady gaze

I Sing of a Man

I sing of a man
Who interred orchids

February two thousand and one
Deadline nearing
For the clearing of Diamond Hill

Before the bulldozers came
In the morning
An orchid farmer
Was busy digging
Through the night
Mass graves
For his orchids
Row upon row
Of all colours and shapes
Rare species

He did not want to see
Those lucent petals succulent leaves
Flowers in bloom
Nubile and waiting
Torn apart and crushed
He buried them instead

As always
The earth consoles with closure

Incense Tree
Aquilaria sinensis

Incense root incense fruit
Incense loading at the port:
Groves of incense trees
Lined the harbour once
At Aberdeen.

Joss sticks, agarwood, potions, scents,
Thriving commerce
Export trade
That once was,
Gave "Hong Kong" its name:
Incense Port, and its fame.

Truly fragrant truly harbour,
But not the
Exoticised "fragrant harbour":
Incense Port its true name.

Heung not Hong
Gong not Kong;
In any case
Transliteration into English sounds
Of monosyllabic tonal Chinese
Is alchemy in reverse
Changing all that is gold
Into dross, loss and mockery.

Poachers come on hacking sprees
From China with saws, axes and carts,
Depleting our incense trees
That did thrive in these parts.
Aquilaria sinensis
The Chinese Incense Tree
Is to-day endangered species.

Marching

The people flowed,
Like so much water between gorges,
As they poured through
The main arteries of the city.

It is another July the first.
Under a scorching sun
Hemmed in by towering city blocks
They walked.
There were placards and banners and drums.
People chanted in unison,
Alternating between
"One, two, three,
Down with Article 23" and
"One, two, three,
Down with Tung Chee-hwa".
People from upper windows
Waved and clapped.
A policeman was seen
Chanting along.

Young parents pushed the young in prams.
They said,
One day we will tell him
He was here this day.

An elderly man was failing.
Supporting him, his daughter-in-law
Rang the chauffeur
To bring up the car
And meet them at the next corner.

The young, the old, with friends, family or alone;
The poor, the rich, professionals, workers, others,
They walked:
Each person giving the other space,
United in one purpose,
Five hundred thousand marchers
Moved on without incident,
Unhurried, unruffled, undeterred.

Article 23 of the Basic Law requires the Hong Kong government to enact laws against sedition, subversion, secession and other security issues. The laws proposed by the government, known as the "Article 23 Bill" was hugely unpopular. There was a large turn-out at the march protesting against the Bill on 1 July. Subsequently, the Bill was withdrawn. Regina Yip, Secretary for Security, who passionately advocated the Bill resigned, as did Tung Chee-hwa, the Chief Executive of Hong Kong.

Forty Years to Go

Long before the event
Two parties agreed
The structure in place
Must not be altered

(Contractual terms
Try to fix what in time
Time changes anyway)

This frenetic dynamo of a place
Protean as ever
Stretching this way and that
In multiple dimensions__
Who is to say
This beast of a thousand faces
Would not stretch the next ten
To sixty or more
Or reduce forty
To a mere twenty
Or less?

Skeltonics

Ten years on and what have we got
Good times bad times the lot
The first headman was put on the spot
Up North noticed the snot
And made him trot
The new man a sot he was not
Still he wasn't all that hot
Before the dreaded slot
Everybody said the city would rot
But nothing has gone to pot
Oh no oh no we have not lost the plot

Giants on the Land (Canada 2007)
For Sarah

Times were when you didn't dare look behind,
Fearing you might see something.
Growing up in the Prairies,
Reality check was the far horizon.
Who knows what's out there.
Weird things happen from time to time.
For sure, there are things (beings), out there.

>Over-sized silos
>They call "grain elevators"
>Define the land.
>They say in their thousands once,
>Now there are only hundreds left.

>These great immensities,
>Many painted bright red,
>They dwarf and shrink
>All that is on earth.

They are not aliens
Who convulse your nights,
But those very red giants,
Trudging along
Heaving and lumbering
Crisscrossing each other
Looking for direction
Looking for shelter.

Some keel over,
And die the death
Of a thousand splinters.

Kindred Growth

My cancer cell my own
My very own
Blood of my blood
Cell of my cell
Parthenogenetic birth
Triggered by a glitch
In cellular communication

As the telomeres shorten
Over lengthening time
Hubristic telomerase
Overrules cell's senescence
Heading for endless growth

You take off
As if there's no to-morrow
Thereby devouring all to-morrows
You live with me
You live off me
Voracious volition
Passionate in your rampaging rapacity
Born of me
You cannot replace me
Procreated of me
You do not descend from me
For you shall not survive me

How on Earth . . .

How on earth did they manage
To synchronise it

They passed time together
Presumably

And they met the days
As they came

Were they friends
Or did they just meet

After a freezing night
The Urban Services
Found two female bodies
In a back alley
Lying side by side
On a piece of board
Under layers of newspapers

They had been seen there
For about a week
Looking pale and sickly
They had a little fire
To cook a little rice
Somehow together they died

TSANG Tsou-choi
"The King of Kowloon"

Call him what you will
Postmodern
Eccentric
Or plain nut
Goodman Tsang
Proclaims himself
The King of Kowloon

For decades
He's been scribbling

On pavements
On walls
On anything with a surface

Reams and reams
Of calligraphy
A rough child's hand
Calligraphy none the less

The post postmoderns call it art

A public nuisance
That even our hard-nosed
Governments have tolerated

> My glimpse of a thing undefined
> Through his years of singular effort
> Perhaps speaks of something
> Stilly ineffable
> Not altogether unrefined
>
> As I weakly try out an idea
> Tsang now hobbles
> On crutches
> How much longer
> Will he be scribbling still

A Veteran Talking

We tossed them high into the air
And caught them coming down,
Sliding straight through
The tips of our bayonets.
Babies cry in any case,
But the women, oh, the women,
They made such a racket;
Had to quieten them down:
That was more bayonet practice.

We had our instructions, we had to clear the place.
We got rid of the men first, one way or another.
As for the women, we did our manly thing with them first
Anywhere, behind doorways, in the middle of the streets
Anytime, morning, afternoon, night,
Then we got rid of them, just as efficiently.

It took only a few days
For us to get into a routine.
We did what had to be done:
Shooting, knifing, hanging, burning,
Whatever was necessary to keep order
In a disorderly city.

After about eight weeks
We succeeded in quelling the ruckus.
It was much hard work:
Unending vigilance and continual practice.
Finally the city surrendered.
It was slightly more manageable, for by then
We had cut the population by half or more.

Even so, there was no letting up
For us the Occupying Force.
Unswervingly, we had to keep our cogs oiled,
Our tanks running, our dignity unsoiled.

Homage to Iris Chang, author of The Rape of Nanking *(1997), with much sadness at her early death.*

La Reine Australienne

Over lunch
La reine australienne
Flew off the handle
Upon hearing Australia
Off-handedly put down

A bride of twenty
When her husband
Took her there
And bashed her to pulp

Now forty and whole
She took twenty years
To reassemble herself
How dare anyone belittle
The site of her reconstruction

Darkness at 4 p.m.

A tsunami of black clouds
Rolls over the hills
We drown in darkness

Furious and violent
A coiling dragon
Catches its tail this way and that
Then El Greco's Toledo in transit
Floods Shatin in eerie light

Finally the storm broke
The heavens split open
And engulfed both cities

Three Poems on a Painter's Works

I Stem tides

Stem tides, stop rhyme: your rhyming.
Stay the music of the spheres,
Till swirling strokes make shapes: your timing.

The orchestra of the skies turns florescent,
As intricate geometry breaks into light,
Exploding colours strangely incandescent.

II Thrash the Heavens

Thrash the heavens, winnow the stars,
Let fall a shower of gold.
Descending into the atmosphere,
It becomes the aurora borealis:
Wave upon wave,
Layer upon layer,
The colours change, shift arabesque
To the music that roars
Like a howling storm.

III You Stand on a Hill Top

You stand on a hill top
And you wave your burning beacon
In gigantic circles
Tempting and teasing
The heavens to descend
They came they came
In vast numbers
In all sizes
The comets the stars the whirling spheres
They danced
They danced on earth
Scraping burning melting it

Dance

Layered surfaces refract the light
From different angles at different times
Translucent colours shimmer and shine
Sashaying with blocks of the opaque

The four dimensions call into account
The hectic traffic
Into and about
Those flat surfaces

And then
Cutting through all that atomic rancour
Rises one clear clean black line
To hold in check
The silence of the spheres

Cock-a-doodle-doo

I sort of sing
Of dinky Kok
Of his aura
In local academia
I sing of him
Tight-arsed
Arse-licking
Potent Kok
Who holds court
Everyday
Over breakfast
In the Kun-ki Club
Dispensing
And receiving
Favours
Now fawning
Now menacing
Whatever's needed
In skullduggery
In a world
Desensitised to
Chicanery

About Turn

About turn
Given our orders
We turned

Reversion marks
Not a turning
But a returning

The turn of a verse
A sleight of hand
Two nations
Each taking turns
To turn us round
Leaving us
With many a confounding turn

In the end
We turned inside out
And that was the end
Of all that turning

Dusk

'Tis the witching hour
Though not mid-night
The hour of entre chien et loup
When light plays with shade
The entr'acte between birth and death
Which we call life
Reduced to an instant
One spot
Which one can just skip across
And be done with

Is it a kind of
Circadian hitch
That catches
Like an electric shock
A sudden inexplicable blackness
A second's deep despair

In a while
The moon rises
Dark branches
Lace the skies
Night has arrived
And all is well

Askew

Sit here
And address the Pacific horizon
Then circumscribe the view
In 360 degrees

Feed the magpies
And hear them
Sing and yodel

Watch the trees
As they filigree the azure
With their foliage

Earth smells sweet
Even time loses
Its sting up here

Then why does the back clamp tight
Guts get tied in knots
The stomach curdles
And sight turns inwards
In an all-consuming repugnance
For all that is or is not

Sounds

Low amplitude high frequency
Rumbling crackle
Throughout the undergrowth

Trees are not ablaze
Air is smokeless
Wherefore the sound of forest fire

Thickly among the pines
Black cockatoos
Feasting busily on acorns
Play a pizzicato of burning

Nests

Pulsating white bodies
Pumping up and down
Like so many hearts

Each white thing
Sequestered in its
Hexagonal chamber
They pump away collectively

Cut to the quick
By Baygon
Some fall off
Others just die

Another wasp nest
For the collection

Notes

Eliot has said it
Free verse is never free
Whoever utters verse
Utters a line
In tune with
The rise and fall of speech
And is
Slotted into measure
Speech stress and metric accent
Combine in counterpoint
Towards rhythmic pattern
In ways
That are perhaps informal
Irregular incidental
Or just found
If verse at all
It is organised speech
Then the reading voice
Renders the fabric
Of words phrases clauses
Weaving together sense and sound
As the poem's cadenced form
Begins to unfold
"Vers libre is in fact vers libéré"

Learning to Walk

Big oaf
Waddling about
Falling off centre
Wrong footing it
Side to side
Front to back
In all directions
Trying to get a hold
Onto something somewhere
Anything anywhere
Nowhere

Until I lose some girth
And walk with precision
I shall not dazzle you
With angled rooms
Built Escher-like
With algebra
That fleshes out
Even zero

In the meantime
Make space
Allow time
Let my foot-fall approach
Give it passage
On the open road
Listen
Say, some even tread yet?

A Poem Is an Object

A poem is an object, what.
How you approach it, that's
Your subjective stance.

Trouble is
Most hover over and about it
Like an obstacle.
They do not read through
To penetrate, with attention
To reveal the object
As dynamic structure,
Language mechanism
Defined by the poem.

All art requires an
Educated response.
Your proverbial
"Man in the street"
May not know that.
(Don't tell him
He doesn't know,
He may bite).

A Poem Is Like

A poem is like
Lightning followed by thunder
Magma bursting forth
Silent rumble of plate tectonics
Geo-politics in a nut-shell
Molecules dancing
Chromosomes behaving
Microbes on a corpse
The Mobius strip
The mathematician's nought
Théophile Gautier's marble
"The other side of silence"
The crossing of parallel lines
"Etcetera"

A poem is always
Controlled language formation
Complex as matter
Simple as a flower
Conditioned
As autonomous
Among infinite variables

It is designed discourse

Curtain Call

Valorous fruit of primordialism
Home grown from erstwhile survivalism

The dust of settler society
Have become pearls of Cultural Piety

Your Identity still in the making
Inspiration everywhere for the taking

The burden of History is here and now
Then comes on Heritage to take its bow

O Brave New World let your Battlers arise
For your daily lives to Mythologize

Found Items

I

Sound of scraping metal
As dried leaves scatter
And strafe the tarmac
Of my garden path

II

Confronting emptiness
It becomes tangible
I conjure up figures
Walking with their heads under their arms

III

Far-flung and isolated
Hemmed in by land and sea

Great continent little room
Vast expanse pocket mind
Scale-cringed and stone-flawed

Here be genius

IV

Under moonlight
In the throes of stillness
I wait
For Caliban's brother to appear

V

In a birthday card
She called him
My friend my God my king

He spear-threw her
Over the cliffs
Near Sydney Harbour

At the morgue
He asked the attendant
Do you mind
If I looked
At her tits

VI

Years ago she jubilantly exclaimed
My mother has read this book
"Thirty Pieces of Silver"
Oh, she knows all about you now

She's got you all sorted out
Aw you're all the same
The Chinese

To-day five acclaimed Australian sinologists
Stride out
From a page of the Higher Education supplement
Fitzgerald
Finnane
Makeham
Barme
Dutton

I should add her mother's name

VII

I froze when she said
I am a Victorian
Was she saying
She was dated or dead

It took me
Almost a second
To realize
She was from Melbourne, Victoria

How tedious
To always having to say
Victorian, I mean Victorian England

The Other Day

The other day
I used a sledge hammer
To kill an ant

This happens
Living here
In these parts

Sun scorched land lost
Purblind
I lose
My cardinal points

Where are the tonalities
Of modified colours
Where are the varied palettes
Of older societies

Ad hoc Australia
Has somersaulted
Over two hundred years
It can only look forward

Those strong of arm
Heart and mind
Will nonetheless garner
The dew of civility
From raw hide

Afterword

Louise Ho: An Afterword[1]

Here is one of the poems included in this collection, a favourite of anthologists.

Home to Hong Kong

A Chinese
Invited an Irishman
To a Japanese meal
By the Spanish Steps
In the middle of Rome
Having come from Boston
On the way home.

The poem attracts attention not on account of any intellectual complexity or emotional intensity, nor for any particularly original or beautiful use of language. Its appeal consists, I think, in an image or story of a Chinese cosmopolitanism, apparently available to Hong Kong people though still, in the 1970s when the poem was written, not much more than a dream to most mainland Chinese. It exercises a kind of flourish, grounded by a cumulative structure that resembles that of a joke. The act of invitation in the main verb of its only sentence is one that places the inviter in the position of host, at home, wherever the invitation is actually issued. It is a cosmopolitan speech act. Here is a life of international friendship, of eclectic taste, of frictionless mobility between scholarly, spiritual, and commercial centres, old world and new, East and West. The poem, like the traveller, is in circulation, beginning and ending at "home", with the only end-rhyme anticipating the bump of arrival, the return to the starting place, laden with each line's trophy of experience or traveller's tale. What could be more desirable, simpler, or

---

1. This afterword is based on a longer essay, "Locating Louise Ho: The place of Hong Kong poetry in English", in *Critical Zone 3* (Hong Kong: Hong Kong University Press, 2008).

more fun? "Home" underwrites the poem, as homecoming underwrites the travelling. Local belonging is the ground for global mobility and gives it a shape.

But what happens when location is not the subject of a statement, but of a question? Such is the odd history of Hong Kong that it used to be quite common to meet a disbelief that the place could be thought of as home. It was a city of exiles, populated by people who had come, for the most part, from the mainland of China in search of business opportunities or political refuge, and the wind that had blown them to the colony might just as easily carry them further in due course, to other cities in Southeast Asia, to North America or Australia. Hong Kong was a transit camp of the Chinese diaspora, a city of sojourners, economic migrants and refugees, and not a place to develop sentimental ties. From the point of view of the Chinese mainland, it was hard to imagine people feeling at home in a modern Chinese city that, however rich, differed from other Chinese cities in being the colonial possession of a foreign power, won by force and legitimated by unequal treaty. Yet from the colonized Chinese city an identity out of difference began to take shape, or take place, a difference from *both* the colonial *and* the national culture, even as 1997 approached and reminders pressed in on us that the colony's days were exactly numbered.

Something of the fragility of this position is signalled in Louise Ho's pre-1997 poem, "Living on the Edge of Mai Po Nature Reserve". The location, in Hong Kong's northern "New Territories" near the Chinese border, is quite specific, and the scene opens in the mode of pastoral.

> This garden this stream these marshes
> A bird sanctuary among the mangroves,
> Herons perch egrets glide,
> The hills gather from afar.

The place of nature is protected from history; nothing happens here. The scene is set with no verbs at all, then traversed by the intransitive activities of herons, egrets, and hills. This first impression is deceptive, however. Within sight of this enclave are shadows of city blocks, and at night "a long row of lights like jewels" marks the electrified high fence — "our Berlin Wall" — separating the colony from mainland China. The line of lights written across the landscape is also a sentence, in the future tense, pointing to the reclamation of Hong Kong, and the "gathering" of the hills in the first stanza starts to emerge into transitivity as the landscape reveals its animate and political meanings (for to gather means to cluster, but also to scoop up). The poem ends like this.

> The horizon closes in like two long arms.
> We are surrounded,
> China holds us in an immense embrace.
> Merely the lie of the land.

This is the first we have heard in the poem of "us", the locals of this locality, now present as the passive victims, or beneficiaries, of being where they are. The edginess of this poem seems to capture a very characteristic divided state of mind in the years leading up to the transfer of sovereignty in 1997, years when the nation over the border impended increasingly over everyday life in Hong Kong. The horizon — the future — is felt as claustrophobic, but may also be sheltering. "Surrounded" is ominous, but "embrace" is reassuring — but then "an immense embrace" seems out of scale for a gesture of maternal solace, and is, besides, not something open to dissent. Who wants, or could refuse, to be held in an *immense* embrace? The tropes applied to the inanimate landscape of the scene begin to stir into a story, and a disquieting one; living on the edge of Mai Po Nature Reserve is indeed living on the edge. The poem's last line — "Merely the lie of the land" — seems reassuring. Don't worry, it seems to say, this is just a poem about scenery. But the ending does not take the edge off the poem. There is, after all, the worrying ambiguity of "the lie of the land", which could indicate simply topography — this is just the way the contours run, no reason to read anything more into it — but also contains a hint of duplicity. And if the look of the peaceful prospect is a lie, what is it lying about? Denial, a classic defensive trope, often draws attention towards what it wants not to see.

There is, however, a world elsewhere, and a third poem, "Migratory", reaches for it uncertainly.

> I floated alone in my king-size bed
> I steered between abysses . . .

This is travel of a different sort from the sociable globetrotting of "Home to Hong Kong", for this time the journey is isolating, alienating, and sounds dangerous, even in fantasy form. It is the journey of exile, its destination Australia, and despite the new immigrant's dutifully taking note of "new shapes new sounds / And endless possibilities", the glance is drawn backwards, inevitably, to locations left behind.

> At first the heart longs
> For the absent familiar
> Cosmopolitan Hong Kong

We can listen to the way the poem tries to console its losses by a nostalgic reverie of being once more at home in the world, travelling effortlessly in memory between favourite places ("Just reeling off their names is ever so comfy", to appropriate Auden), in a sort of global freedom like that enjoyed in "Home to Hong Kong". But that cosmopolitanism was anchored and guaranteed by the local groundedness from which it departed, to which it would return; and here in "Migratory", as the title had warned, that groundedness is no longer a given.

> O land, walk with me
> May the dust settle
> Wherever I may stand.

Dislocation makes necessary relocation and this makes possible, though it does not guarantee, a new and much more difficult kind of freedom, one that is not given but made. In "Migratory" we see it establish a narrow and precarious foothold, where the home lost or abandoned is replaced by a more abstract location, a subject position, wherever the subject pronoun makes a stand. But in this move, "Migratory" is characteristic of Louise Ho's poetry as a whole. For the Hong Kong poet of her generation, who has known a Hong Kong colonized, internationalized, globalized, decolonized, and renationalized, locality — a place to belong to — has always been something to be created, brought into being, through writing. Writing is a way of finding your feet.

Louise Ho is, of course, a Chinese poet who finds her feet in English. She appears more than happy to work with a language that might be thought a colonial residue, or a cargo of inappropriate and distorting associations, without seeking (as some other English-using poets have) to purge it of its traditions. On the contrary she relishes the chance to make use of these traditions, sometimes to make fun of them. At times she uses Cantonese words or sounds within her English poems (as in the macaronic "Jamming", with its carnivalesque Cantonese nonsense-refrain, "geeleegulu"), and describes one of her goals as the creation of "a space where the English literary language expresses as well as is incorporated into the local ethos, thus becoming almost a *tertium quid*, but which remains at the same time definitely English".[2] Meanwhile, while certainly oriented outward to international readers and outlets, she is from beginning to end a poet of Hong Kong experience and history. And while hers is certainly not the kind of work readily harnessed to nation-building projects or a national moral and aesthetic agenda, nor is it shaped by a rejection of local aesthetic and linguistic practices, especially as embodied in Cantonese. The poem "Well-spoken Cantonese" describes an eloquent man, and ends like this:

His modulated resonance
Creates a civilized space

---

2. Louise Ho, "Hong Kong writing and writing Hong Kong", *Hong Kong English: Autonomy and Creativity*, ed. Kingsley Bolton (Hong Kong: Hong Kong University Press, 2002), 173–82; 176.

Or a proper silence
Which was not there
Before he spoke.

The medium of written English and the subject of Cantonese speech collaborate, as it were, to make "a civilized space". Language builds the city. It also furnishes the city's memorial, its memory of past lives and deaths.

The shadows of June the fourth
Are the shadows of a gesture,
They say, but how shall you and I
Name them, one by one?

The poem "Remembering 4th June, 1989" asks difficult questions about memory, the memory of the national crisis named in its title, and it does so in an inflection set by Hong Kong and by English. In this, it is another episode in this poet's long commentary on the history of her own times and places, stretching back to two poems about the Hong Kong riots of 1967, and commemorating cultural, demographic, and architectural changes, besides events such as the 1997 handover itself, and more recent changes in the city's ethos and its streets. It is a historical record, the poetry being witness to a changing structure of feeling in a place which has been, whatever else, both unique and exemplary as the site of so many of the shaping forces of modern times. Characteristically, canonical English poetry is invoked here to assist in *seeing* and understanding the memory of 4 June 1989. The spirits of Dryden, Marvell and Yeats are summoned into the poem from the traditional canon of English Literature. But they are also the three greatest political poets in English, each with an intimate experience of self-divided communities and civil unrest. English poetry has a history of thinking about political power and opposition to it, which is activated in the way this poem triangulates Marvell, Dryden and Yeats, thus creating an intellectual location which can be in effect a standpoint, or footing, a *locus standi*. A history inscribed in the words and names of

160

English provides this other place, within the poem, from which its topic — remembering 4 June 1989 — can be contemplated.

For the Hong Kong poet as for the English (and Irish) poets in their time, the question is how a poet ought to respond to, name, and remember, a desperate moment in history, arousing painful and divided emotions as it happens, and bringing consequences — like a stone cast into water, in Yeats's image — whose implications will take a long time to ripple out from the centre. The focus of the poem is not so much on China as on Hong Kong itself, and on the way events over the border catalyzed, in the territory divided and uncertain and anxious about its own future, a sense of itself as a single community.

> As we near the end of an era
> We have at last
> Become ourselves . . .

This moment of becoming does not crystallize into a political resolution (it's hard to see where the agency for such a resolution could have come from for Hong Kong people in 1989) but is an awareness that was not fully there before. The problem of 4 June and its aftermath for people in Hong Kong was a problem of where to stand.

> We have lived
> By understanding
>
> Each in his own way
> The tautness of the rope
> Underfoot.

The intelligence, poise and integrity of poems like Yeats' "Easter 1916" and Marvell's "Horatian Ode" have played a part in bringing this predicament into visibility. Nonetheless it is quite specific, a moment of Hong Kong autobiography. The tightrope is an uncomfortable location, yet suited to Hong Kong's "genius" — a predicament, but also a performance, the balances and the turns in which Hong Kong's future will be played out in the open.

Questions of location, of standing or footing, keep coming back in many of Louise Ho's more recent poems. For her these issues are often entangled with questions of artistic form, as in a poem like "About Turn" which is about poetic as well as political turns and returns; but they are just as likely to surface in her comic and satiric poems. The Australian poems in particular have a fascinated unease about them. There is in them a secular version of what T. S. Eliot meant, I think, by the phrase "the spirit unappeased and peregrine", here taking the form of a mobile, restless intelligence and an unillusioned eye. It is an eye trained to pick out the grotesque — the comic grotesque of "Cock-a-doodle-doo", or the tragic grotesque of the street sleepers of "How on earth . . ." with their coincidental death. But it is also capable of the kind of reflection — which can mean imitation, but also thinking — that, in the poem which opens this book, reveals an unromantic but lucid epiphany.

> Not being Narcissus
> The self does not dissipate
>
> Watch how pool upon pool
> The water grows limpid
> Under your steady gaze.

These poems are a record of where, over some forty years, that travelling gaze has settled.

Douglas Kerr
Professor, Department of English
Hong Kong University

162

Appendices

Introductory remarks to "Sheung Shui Pastoral 1977"

The Hong Kong Arts Centre has organized yearly poetry-readings since 1974 and one of the more prominent poets taking part has been [Louise] S. W. Ho. Her poems have always been received with great enthusiasm, especially for their concentration and clarity.

Although of Chinese origin, her medium of expression is English and in her poems she achieves a subtle synthesis of her Chinese environment and her Western education. When she was still studying at the English Department of Hong Kong University her poems were already noted for their outstanding quality. They show the mastery of language in expressing and reflecting Hong Kong through her own reaction to it.

The Hong Kong Arts Centre is pleased to announce the publication of this selection of poems by [Louise] S. W. Ho.

Helga Burger-Werle
October 1977
Programme Manager
The Hong Kong Arts Centre

Introduction to "Local Habitation" Dialect without a Tribe[1]

It has always seemed to me that Werner Herzog's film *Fitzcarraldo* has a special appeal for those of us living in Hong Kong. *Fitzcarraldo* tells a story about a crazy Irishman (played — why not? — by the German actor Klaus Kinski) and his attempts to build an opera house in the midst of the Amazon jungles in Peru. It is an enterprise that involves among other things moving a heavy boat over a mountain. We can leave aside Fitzcarraldo's exploitation of the natives, or Herzog's method of filmmaking which it is said spoiled the region for other filmmakers and ethnographers, and focus for the time being on the film's mythic dimension. It is not the philosophic myth of Sisyphus that we find, but something else: an urban myth about desire and obsession. As such, the myth can serve as a superb hyperbole for Hong Kong cultural life, because in this city — "that last emporium" — it is obsession that brings skylines or poetic lines into being. What Louise Ho writes in "Raw" might have been spoken by Fitzcarraldo:

> Raw as an open wound that insists
> On the extremity of pain
> In order t o reach fulfillment
> Is every desire

And it matters little whether it is desire for philately or philandering, for askesis or acquisition. In certain situations, to get anything done at all requires extreme measures.

---

1. This has subsequently appeared as part of a chapter in *Hong Kong: Culture and Politics of Disappearance*, by Ackbar Abbas (Minneapolis: University of Minnesota Press, 1997).

The extremities in Louise Ho's poetry are masked initially by what seems to be a reliance on English Literature as a form of poetic authority. From the title of her volume, *Local Habitation*, to many details of phrasing, echoes of Shakespeare, the Metaphysicals and the Moderns are everywhere. However, it soon becomes apparent that the references to English Literature are there not to show her cultural credentials or to prove that she has earned the right to write in English. English Literature figures in Louise Ho's work somewhat like the *Don Quixote* figures in Pierre Menard's. It is never a question of working in English Literature but rather of re-working the literature. That is why even if the allusions are to English, their meanings get changed by the new context they find themselves in. For example, the project suggested in the title of portraying the city by giving to airy nothing a local habitation and a name works itself out in unexpected ways. In poem after poem, it is the very attempt at naming and precision that *reveals* the frayed edges of a city where nothing is but what is not. This can take a humorous form, as in "What's in a Name", about the city's incongruous sounding name when transliterated into English from Chinese:

> I whispered it
> I insinuated it
> only as acronym.
> For it rhymed too well
> with ting tong sing song
> King Kong and ping pong

Or it can take a more serious turn, as in the poem about the Tiananmen Massacre, which begins by invoking Marvell, Dryden and Yeats, and modulates quickly into the problem of naming:

> The shadows of June the fourth
> Are the shadows of a gesture,
> They say, but how shall you and I
> Name them, one by one?

In poems like these, English Literature is an initial point of departure that allows the poet to take her bearings on local life and politics, both of which are becoming increasingly elusive and hard to describe. English Literature functions less as a form of poetic authority than as a grid from situating the metastasizing habitations of the local.

The fact that Louise Ho chooses to write in English is not in itself a remarkable fact, given Hong Kong's status as a still-British colony. What is remarkable — her form of extremity — is that the cultural, political and personal tensions of the city are so precisely focused by the tensions of her language, by the sensation of "The tautness of the rope / Underfoot." For the use of English in Hong Kong by a non-native speaker is subject to multiple social tensions and difficulties. The non-native can try to minimalize these multiplicities by mimicking the accents and idioms of the native speaker, and hide behind conventionalities. It is always language, more so than conscience, that makes cowards of us all. Or she can choose to explore and exploit these multiplicities and differences, and risk misunderstanding or even polite derision. It is in this social and linguistic space in between the conventional and the inchoate that Louise Ho's texts can be situated. The poet, she writes in "Poetry Is Never of Emotion", is someone

> Who shuffles from kitchen to loo
> Biting his nails not knowing what to do.

In "Jamming", more challengingly and interestingly and also more typical of her best work, the very uncertainties of this space-in-between are worked into a bravura linguistic performance. In the process, a Cantonese slang word is introduced (as a refrain) into poetry in English:

> Ooooh, do you think
> she can tell the difference
> Between irony and mere cliché
> geeleegulu

To the demand that our language should always be judged by the standards of the native speaker, the only proper reply is — geeleegulu. The word is Cantonese slang for linguistic confusion, and functions in the poem as a way of shrugging off the anxiety of correctness, in order to do something different in English:

> Bacon didn't trust it much
> But Churchill thought it rather grand
> On these our very own shores
> Let us make our very own
> geeleegulu

For Louise Ho, writing cannot be a matter of purifying the dialect of the tribe which might have been a valid aspiration for a Frenchman of the nineteenth century or even for an Anglophile American from Kansas City. It cannot be an aspiration for someone in Hong Kong.

Many of the poems in the volume deal with aesthetic themes, but the aesthetic covers a wide spectrum of emotions and implications. It ranges from a simple admiration for the beauty of form in people and objects, in poems like "After Yeats", "Jade", "Moma"; to a more complex note about the insufficiency of beauty, as in "Soliloquy of a White Jade Brooch" ("she loved / My white viscosities", but then "she discarded me / For the other / Complex design"); and finally to a more marked sense of the responsibility of form. It is at this point that the aesthetic begins to shade into the political. Thus a poem like "Canticle on a Drop of Water" might read like a format exercise in the style of John Donne:

> Like a drop of water the will
> Hovers above without contact,
> Adjacent to but always detached from
> Its limbeck which is the soul . . .

— but the poetic conceit of "hovering water-drop / will" gives, however indirectly, a better sense of the floating realities of social and political life in Hong Kong than what we can read in an overtly political poem like "Remembering 4th June, 1989". Similarly, the poem that captures best the political tensions and ambiguities of the city is perhaps "Bronze Horse", which restricts itself to a careful description of an art object, a very striking piece of sculpture by Mak Hin Yeung. The sculpture depicts a horse's legs "flaying the air" and the human legs dangling from the pedestal. This is not a centaur, image of wisdom achieved through the reconciliation of animality and humanity, but a mindless image of violence and obscenity in which no terrible beauty is born:

> Two motions clash
> like trains
> into each other's velocity,
> two bodies
> countermining,
> two contraries
> forced into one orbit:
> the unseen body
> fully in control,
> meets the unseen head,
> losing control,
> at the neck
> of a bronze horse.

It is not necessary to translate the image into a political allegory critical of the slogan "one country, two systems". The form can speak for itself.

If form mediates the political in Louise Ho's work, linking language to the city, it also mediates the personal, linking public to private life. This can be read most clearly in those poems where the figure of the mother is an overwhelming presence. For example, a poem about writing can turn into a poem about birth and the mother, partly because writing is also a way of confronting one's own personal history. The poet, Louise Ho writes, is "a large collection of images", but then

> These do not make a picture.
> The images are scattered by constant change,
>   are not connected.

What lurks in the hollows
Between time and time?
An absence of adhesion
Like mother's love perhaps . . .

We do not have to "psychoanalyse" the image of the mother in these lines. All we have to note is that poetic forms ("images") and the forms of public and private life all share the same quality: a lack of cohesion. History, as Roland Barthes said somewhere, is related to hysteria (from *hyster:* the womb). History as hysteria is what these personal poems adumbrate for us. It is a history that does not present itself as a coherent, cohesive narrative and does not follow clear structural rules. The initial moments of such a history are mired in confusion, even self-loathing:

My nine-months' mother's womb,
With no menstrual issuance,
Blew up with slimy green black bracken,
To grind me out at birth
A deformed lump.

("Time's Pummelling")

At the end of the process, if one is lucky, a subject may be formed:

Gestation took decades
In the end
it nearly killed me.

("I Love the Child in Me")

The poems in *Local Habitation*, benefit from being read together, but not for the banal reason that they then add up to a greater whole. On the contrary, it is only when we read these poems as a collection that we begin to see their uncompromising fragmentariness. They are like snapshots of a disappearing landscape. There are no grand odes, only episodes. The story is not over yet.

Ackbar Abbas*
Professor, Department of Comparative Literature
Hong Kong University

---

* Ackbar Abbas is currently Professor of Comparative Literature in the School of Humanities at the University of California, Irvine.

Introduction to "New Ends, Old Beginnings 1997"

The title of Louise Ho's superb new collection of poems wrings the neck of a cliché. The commonplace "new beginnings" has been inverted and thereby subverted: what results, appropriately enough for a collection of poems about Hong Kong's future, is radical uncertainty.

Eliot's "In my end is my beginning" floats into the mind, and Ho reveals herself as a modernist rather than a post-modernist poet, in whom echoes of Eliot and Yeats and Auden are often to be heard.

But what if we take "ends" in its other major sense? The implications are even more unsettling. Susan Sontag has remarked of Walter Benjamin that his sentences "do not intend". What can we make of non-intentional sentences, utterances, poems, in relation to the prosaic everyday means and ends of politics and history?

Ho's poems here chart an Odyssey towards such a sensibility. She starts out under the regime of the "old ends" with some kind of classical antithesis: her first group of poems includes two that appear in sharp contradiction — one about the pro-China, anti-British riots of 1967, and the other about the Democracy movement and its suppression in 1989. In this world, there is an apparently reassuring sense of limits and borders — trains seem to come to *their* end at the Chinese University of Hong Kong, and there is an apparently clear border between China and Hong Kong at the Mai Po Nature Reserve.

But this Odysseus then embarks on a journey "into exile" in Australia which vastly enriches and complicates her poetic language. It is an encounter with the strangeness of all language, as well as with the poet's complexly-layered relationship with the English language in particular. She listens in the silence, and hears strange sounds from birds and beasts. She confronts what she hears with a profoundly original sense of humour. Elsewhere, she hears the wonderful diphthongs in the Australian pronunciation of "o", and registers the prosaic English "home" as "heaoaium".

"Heaoaium", she learns in Australia, is nowhere: Hong Kong is a "floating island", and Australia a place of radical impermanence for her. At the same time, however, the emptiness of Australia seems to increase her capacity to take on "big" subjects. Like another Chinese poet, Mao Tse Tung, she likes to play with images of size, juxtaposing "little" Hong Kong — "this compact commercial enclave" — with "big" China. And amongst the "big" subjects she now tackles are two that are essential for the public poet reflecting upon July 1997 and the like: time and history.

Though she obviously feels that she doesn't fit into the modern, ad hoc, Australia, she wonders who is really at home in this place — no one, it seems, except Aboriginal people.

Thereafter the poet return to Hong Kong, upon who she calls with renewed power to confront its multiplicities. Back in Hong Kong she is now (at least) French, Australian, Chinese, Mauritian, colonist and colonized, English and above all Cantonese. Though it's the English persona, perhaps, that know most about "The varying declensions / Of layered self-deprecation / The sleight of hand". From a deeper layer of the self comes a prophetic warning of potential disaster in Hong Kong's future.

Louise Ho is a strongly visual poet. She finds a powerful image for the complex process of metamorphosis that July 1997 means to her in Mak Hin Yeung's sculptured "Bronze Horse", where a horse's torso and a human torso coalesce — both of them headless. This "end of era or change of chapter" is negotiated in poems of all shapes and sizes, apparently "big" and apparently "small", such as the pregnant "At the Crossroads", in which three paths point the way forward.

Ho reflects in these poems Thomas Mann's "pathos of the middle" — that ironic sense of historical perspective that realizes that knowledge of absolute beginnings and absolute ends can never be had by beings essentially immersed in time. She illuminates and exemplifies many paradoxes, including the strange one that seems to decree that nowadays so much of the sustaining of the Western tradition seems to be done by non-Westerners, and so much reinventing of the culture of the colonizers by the apparently colonized.

She is a cosmopolitan sophisticate with a saving dose of simplicity. Would that the introduction of the euro might find a laureate with half the vision and wisdom and sense of fun that Louise Ho applies to July 1997.

Michael Hollington
Professor of English at the University of New South Wales,
Australia, and the University of Toulon and of Var, France